UI UX Design

"A Middle-Level Guide to Integrating Aesthetics with Functionality in Interface Design"

Brian Peel

Table of Contents

Introduction

Recap of Beginner Concepts

In the field of UI/UX design, mastering the basic principles is essential before progressing to more advanced topics. This overview revisits the foundational elements critical to every UI/UX designer's education, emphasizing how these basic concepts underpin effective, efficient, and sophisticated design.

Differentiating UI from UX

Understanding the difference between User Interface (UI) and User Experience (UX) is fundamental. UI refers to the physical aspects of a product that a user interacts with, such as its layout, visual elements, and interactive components—akin to the aesthetics and controls in a car. UX, meanwhile, relates to the overall experience of using that product, comparable to the feel of driving the car. UX encompasses how the product meets the user's needs through its design.

Principles of User-Centered Design

User-Centered Design (UCD) advocates for a focus on the user's needs throughout the product development process. This approach involves:

- **Research**: Identifying user characteristics, needs, and behaviors.

- **Design**: Developing solutions that cater to these needs.

- **Testing**: Continuously evaluating design effectiveness and making necessary adjustments based on user feedback.

Establishing Visual Hierarchy and Layout

Creating a visual hierarchy is critical for guiding users through a digital product effectively. This involves strategically arranging elements to signal their importance using size, color, and placement. A well-thought-out visual hierarchy ensures that users naturally gravitate towards the most important information or actions first.

```
.header {
    font-size: 22px;
    color: #444;
}

.subheader {
    font-size: 16px;
    color: #777;
}

.text {
    font-size: 12px;
    color: #aaa;
}
```

Color Theory and Typography in Design

Color and typography are pivotal in setting the tone and enhancing usability. Color influences emotions and actions and should be chosen to align with the goals of the design. Typography impacts how information is processed and perceived. Effective typography promotes readability and user comfort, with considerations for font type, spacing, and hierarchy being key.

Example CSS for typography:

```
body {
    font-family: 'Helvetica', sans-serif;
    line-height: 1.8;
}
```

Navigational Design Principles

Good navigation is vital for a positive UX. It should be intuitive, consistent, and facilitate easy exploration of a website or app. Well-designed navigation helps users find information efficiently and without frustration, utilizing elements like menu bars, search functions, and intuitive layouts.

Utilizing Images and Icons

Images and icons serve as powerful communication tools in UI design, offering a visual method to convey messages quickly and effectively. They should be used thoughtfully to support content and guide user interactions, maintaining simplicity and clarity to avoid overwhelming the user.

Interaction Design Fundamentals

Interaction design is about crafting an engaging interface with logical and responsive interactions. Effective interaction design considers how interactions fit within the entire user journey, emphasizing feedback and usability. For instance, adding interactive feedback such as button hover effects can enhance the user experience:

```
.button:hover {
    background-color: #e1e1e1;
}
```

Conclusion

Revisiting these fundamental UI/UX design concepts is crucial for solidifying a designer's base of knowledge. Understanding and applying these principles allows for the creation of more user-friendly, intuitive, and attractive digital products. As designers become proficient in these basics, they can more confidently tackle complex design challenges, pushing the boundaries of creativity and innovation in digital design.

Importance of Balancing Aesthetics and Functionality

In UI/UX design, striking a balance between aesthetic appeal and practical functionality is essential. This equilibrium is crucial not just for attracting users but also for ensuring effective interaction with digital products. This article explores the necessity of integrating aesthetic design with functional utility and how this integration can significantly enhance user experiences.

Primary Goals of UI/UX Design

UI/UX design aims to serve two main purposes: capturing user interest through visual elements and facilitating efficient user interactions. While aesthetic features create the initial engagement and set the product's tone, functionality underpins ongoing user satisfaction by enabling straightforward and effective product use.

Aesthetics: Beyond Surface-Level Appeal

Aesthetics in UI/UX design transcend mere attractiveness, setting the stage for user perception and establishing trust in the product's quality. Effective aesthetic design not only pleases the eye but also supports usability, with strategic use of color schemes to improve navigation and carefully chosen typography to aid information processing.

```css
/* CSS for enhancing both visual appeal and user interface efficiency */
.body {
    background-color: #fafafa; /* Gentle background color for ease of viewing */
    color: #333; /* High-contrast text color for better readability */
    font-family: 'Arial', sans-serif; /* Functional yet elegant typography choice */
}
```

Functionality: Core of User Interactions

Functionality is about the practical use of the product: how intuitively users can navigate the interface and how efficiently they can accomplish their objectives. Even the most visually striking design will falter if users struggle with basic tasks due to poor functionality.

Integrating Aesthetics with Functionality

Achieving an optimal integration of aesthetics with functionality involves specific strategies that ensure visual elements and operational performance support each other effectively. Here are some essential strategies:

1. **Unified Design Elements**: Consistency in visual elements enhances not only the interface's beauty but also its usability, making the system easier to learn and interact with.

2. **Simplicity in Design**: Emphasizing simplicity helps in decluttering the interface, which improves both aesthetic quality and navigational ease.

3. **Ongoing User Feedback**: Continuously engaging with users to obtain feedback helps refine both the visual appeal and the functionality of the product.

```javascript
// JavaScript for A/B testing interface options
if (userGroup === 'A') {
    document.getElementById("add-to-cart-button").className = "style-a";
} else {
    document.getElementById("add-to-cart-button").className = "style-b";
}
```

4. **Responsive and Adaptable Design**: Ensuring designs are adaptable across different devices maintains a consistent user experience that is both attractive and functional.

Advantages of a Balanced Design Approach

A product that well balances aesthetics with functionality is more likely to keep users engaged and satisfied, leading to better retention and more frequent use. This balance not only improves the individual user's experience but also enhances the overall brand perception and increases market competitiveness.

Conclusion

Balancing aesthetics with functionality in UI/UX design involves more than just compromise; it requires a deliberate effort to ensure that each enhances the other. This balanced approach is crucial for developing digital products that are both attractive and practical, meeting modern users' high expectations. As UI/UX design evolves, maintaining this balance will continue to be a pivotal skill for designers, ensuring their work effectively meets user needs and stands out in a crowded digital environment.

Overview of Intermediate UI/UX Design Topics

As UI/UX designers progress from foundational to more advanced topics, they encounter a range of intermediate concepts essential for developing more nuanced and effective interfaces. These concepts extend from sophisticated layout adjustments to the nuanced use of color and typography, all tailored to enhance user engagement and interaction. This overview discusses critical intermediate topics that are key to evolving from a beginner to an adept UI/UX designer.

Advanced Layout Techniques

At an intermediate level, UI/UX design involves leveraging complex layout techniques such as Flexbox and CSS Grid, which offer greater flexibility and control compared to basic layouts. These techniques facilitate the creation of adaptive designs that maintain visual integrity and usability across various devices.

Flexbox is ideal for managing layouts with elements of varying dimensions and alignments, providing a streamlined solution to responsive design challenges:

```
.container {
    display: flex;
    flex-direction: row;
    justify-content: space-around;
    align-items: center;
}
```

CSS Grid introduces a two-dimensional layout capability, simplifying the creation of intricate designs that were once dependent on multiple nested structures:

```
.grid-container {
    display: grid;
    grid-template-columns: auto auto auto;
    gap: 15px;
}
```

These advanced techniques empower designers to construct more dynamic and responsive layouts that respond intuitively to user needs.

Color and Visual Psychology

Intermediate UI/UX design requires a deep understanding of how color influences user perception and behavior. Designers learn to apply color psychology effectively to enhance user experience, employing colors that align with the emotional tone of the application while ensuring accessibility.

Typography Beyond the Basics

Beyond choosing appropriate fonts, intermediate typography involves creating a visual hierarchy that guides the user's eye and facilitates information processing. Designers at this stage manage typography to optimize readability and enhance the aesthetic appeal of the interface.

```css
.body-text {
    font-family: 'Roboto', sans-serif;
    font-size: 18px;
    line-height: 1.6;
}

.heading {
    font-family: 'Merriweather', serif;
    font-size: 30px;
    font-weight: bold;
    line-height: 1.2;
}
```

Proper use of typography not only improves usability but also elevates the overall design.

Interactive Elements and Micro-interactions

Developing interactive elements such as hover effects, feedback animations, and other micro-interactions is crucial at the intermediate level. These elements provide subtle cues and enhance the interactive dialogue between the user and the application.

```javascript
document.querySelector('.button').addEventListener('mouseenter', function() {
    this.style.transform = 'scale(1.1)';
});
```

Such micro-interactions enrich the user experience, making interactions not only functional but also engaging.

Advanced Usability Testing

Intermediate designers employ more sophisticated usability testing methods, combining qualitative and quantitative techniques to uncover deeper insights into user behavior and preferences. Tools like eye-tracking technology, in-depth A/B testing, and extensive user feedback systems are integral to refining user interfaces.

```
// Example code for implementing A/B testing
if (userVariant === 'B') {
    document.getElementById("new-feature").style.display = "block";
} else {
    document.getElementById("new-feature").style.display = "none";
}
```

These methods allow for more targeted improvements, ensuring that the design choices are informed by actual user interactions.

Conclusion

Transitioning to intermediate UI/UX design involves a deeper exploration of technical tools and conceptual understanding. Mastery of these intermediate topics enables designers to tackle complex design challenges and push the boundaries of what is possible, ensuring that their creations are not only aesthetically pleasing but also highly functional and aligned with user needs. This level of expertise paves the way for more innovative design solutions and a greater impact on user satisfaction.

Chapter One

Advanced Layout Techniques

Exploring Grid Variations and Flexibility

In the dynamic field of UI/UX design, an in-depth understanding of grid systems and their variations is essential for crafting user-friendly and visually compelling interfaces. Grids provide a structured method for organizing design elements, but with the increasing complexity of digital interfaces, advanced grid configurations become necessary. This article discusses the different types of grid systems available to designers and how these can be customized to better meet the requirements of sophisticated digital environments, including practical examples for implementation.

Advanced Grid Systems Overview

Grids are crucial in design for maintaining order and visual balance. While simple grids suffice for straightforward projects, more complex designs require adaptable and nuanced grid systems:

1. **Modular Grids**: These grids divide the layout space into multiple blocks or modules that can be rearranged or resized, offering designers flexibility in content presentation. Modular grids are especially useful in

projects where diverse content forms need cohesive integration within the layout.

2. **Hierarchical Grids**: Tailored to content significance, these grids do not adhere to a strict uniform structure but are instead designed to elevate primary content visually. They are ideal for interfaces where information priority varies, such as in web pages that combine promotional and informational content.

3. **Baseline Grids**: Essential for text-heavy designs, baseline grids ensure that lines of text across columns align perfectly, significantly enhancing readability and creating a rhythmically consistent user experience.

Implementing Flexible Grids with Modern CSS

The development of CSS technologies like Grid Layout and Flexbox has revolutionized the implementation of complex and responsive grid systems, allowing for greater creativity and control in web design.

CSS Grid Layout

The CSS Grid Layout is a powerful two-dimensional system that simplifies the creation of intricate designs and allows elements to overlap if necessary, offering precise control over both columns and rows.

```
.container {
    display: grid;
    grid-template-columns: repeat(3, 1fr);
    gap: 20px;
    auto-rows: minmax(120px, auto);
}
```

This setup creates a three-column grid with flexible row heights, which adjusts content dynamically and maintains a fixed gap for clarity.

Flexbox

Flexbox provides a more streamlined, one-dimensional layout solution, ideal for managing space distribution within a container when the size of the items is unknown or dynamic.

```css
.container {
    display: flex;
    flex-direction: row;
    justify-content: space-between;
    align-items: center;
}
```

This configuration organizes items horizontally, evenly distributing space around them and aligning them centrally, suitable for a variety of layout patterns.

Key Considerations in Advanced Grid Usage

Adopting advanced grid systems requires careful consideration of several factors:

- **Content Hierarchy**: The grid design must reflect the importance of the content, ensuring that key information is prominently displayed.

- **Responsive Design**: It's crucial for grids to be responsive, adapting effectively across different screen sizes to ensure consistency and functionality.

- **Cross-Browser Compatibility**: Ensuring that grid layouts perform uniformly across various browsers is essential, possibly requiring the use of specific prefixes or fallback strategies.

Conclusion

Advanced grid systems are invaluable for UI/UX designers looking to tackle complex design challenges. By mastering the use of various grid variations and learning to adapt them for flexible, responsive layouts, designers can enhance the aesthetics and functionality of their digital products. As technology and user needs evolve, the ability to innovate within grid configurations remains a critical skill in the designer's toolkit, ensuring that digital interfaces are both attractive and efficient.

Dynamic Layouts for Different Devices

In today's tech-driven world, UI/UX designers must ensure their layouts are versatile across a multitude of devices. This adaptability is essential for user engagement and consistent functionality regardless of the device. This discussion outlines methods for designing layouts that dynamically adapt to various screen sizes and orientations, showcasing coding examples to illustrate these approaches.

Core Principles of Responsive Design

Responsive design hinges on key principles that facilitate fluid transitions between diverse device displays:

- **Fluid Grids**: By employing relative rather than fixed units, these grids allow design elements to adjust fluidly to the screen size.

- **Flexible Images and Media**: This principle ensures that media elements scale effectively within different container sizes, preserving their quality and relevance.

- **Media Queries**: These CSS rules enable the application of unique styles based on specific device features such as display type, width, and orientation.

CSS Strategies for Adaptive Layouts

Several CSS techniques are pivotal in crafting layouts that are responsive and easily adjustable, including Flexbox, CSS Grid, and media queries.

Flexbox

Flexbox facilitates an efficient way to layout, align, and distribute space among items in a container, regardless of their size, making it invaluable for responsive design.

```
.container {
    display: flex;
    flex-direction: row;
    justify-content: space-between;
    align-items: flex-start;
}
```

This Flexbox setup ensures items within the container adjust their spacing and alignment effectively, enhancing responsiveness.

CSS Grid

CSS Grid supports sophisticated, two-dimensional layouts that remain robust and flexible across various screen sizes.

```css
.grid-container {
    display: grid;
    grid-template-columns: repeat(auto-fill, minmax(120px, 1fr));
    gap: 15px;
}
```

This grid configuration automatically adjusts the number of columns to fit the container's width, allowing the design to respond seamlessly to changes in screen size.

Media Queries

Media queries are essential for adapting layouts to different environmental conditions by applying specific CSS modifications.

```css
@media (max-width: 500px) {
    .container {
        flex-direction: column;
    }
}
```

This media query changes the container's direction to a column layout when the screen width is less than 500 pixels, optimizing it for smaller screens.

Addressing Responsive Design Challenges

Responsive design presents challenges such as ensuring compatibility across devices and optimizing performance:

- **Cross-Device Compatibility**: It is critical that designs function flawlessly on all devices, necessitating extensive testing and specific adjustments.

- **Performance Optimization**: Optimizing for varied device capabilities and connection speeds is crucial. Techniques like adaptive images and lazy loading are beneficial, especially on mobile.

Designers can enhance performance by:

- Employing responsive image techniques that adjust image resolutions based on the device, improving load times and conserving bandwidth.

- Implementing asynchronous loading to prioritize critical content and enhance the speed of initial page loads.

Conclusion

Dynamic layouts are fundamental in contemporary UI/UX design, enabling designers to create interfaces that are visually appealing and functionally robust on any device. Advanced CSS tools such as Flexbox, CSS Grid, and media queries are instrumental in making designs adaptable and user-friendly. As device diversity continues to expand, mastering these responsive design techniques becomes increasingly vital for delivering exceptional user experiences across the digital landscape.

Balancing Aesthetic Appeal with Usability

In the field of UI/UX design, achieving a balance between aesthetic appeal and functional usability is paramount. This equilibrium is vital as it impacts initial user attraction and long-term usability of the interface. An interface that is visually attractive can draw users in, while its usability ensures their continued engagement. This article will discuss how to integrate aesthetic appeal with practical usability, including examples of coding techniques that aid this balance.

Importance of Aesthetic Appeal

Aesthetic appeal plays several critical roles in UI/UX design:

- **Creating Immediate Impact**: The visual design of an interface is typically the first interaction a user has with a product. Effective design can captivate users instantly, setting the stage for further interaction.

- **Reflecting Brand Identity**: The visual elements of a product communicate the brand's ethos and values. Consistent visual themes such as color schemes, typography, and imagery help to reinforce the brand and enhance user recall.

- **Boosting Engagement**: An aesthetically pleasing design can make the user experience more enjoyable, potentially increasing the likelihood of users staying longer within the application or website.

While aesthetics are crucial, they should enhance rather than hinder the functionality of the product.

Significance of Usability

Usability ensures that an interface is accessible and efficient for a broad range of users:

- **Simplicity of Use**: The design should allow new users to intuitively navigate the interface without extensive guidance.

- **Efficiency of Interaction**: For regular users, the design should facilitate a quick and easy way to perform tasks, enhancing user productivity.

- **Universal Accessibility**: Design considerations should include features that make the interface accessible to all users, including those with disabilities, ensuring compliance with accessibility standards.

Strategies for Harmonizing Aesthetics and Usability

Balancing visual appeal with functionality involves strategic design and thoughtful implementation. Here are key strategies to achieve this harmony:

1. Visual Hierarchy

A clearly defined visual hierarchy can guide users effortlessly to the most important information or actions.

```css
/* CSS to enhance visual hierarchy */
h1 {
    font-size: 26px;
    color: #333;
}
p {
    font-size: 14px;
    color: #666;
}
```

This CSS effectively differentiates between headings and body text, aiding user navigation through the visual structure of the content.

2. Functional Aesthetics

Visual elements should not only decorate but also serve functional purposes. For example, color coding can intuitively guide users about what actions are safe or potentially risky.

```css
/* Styling for functional color cues */
.cancel-button {
    background-color: #e74c3c;
}
.proceed-button {
    background-color: #2ecc71;
}
```

This coding uses red for a cancel button and green for a proceed button, leveraging colors as functional elements that aid decision-making.

3. Responsive Designs

Ensure that designs adapt effectively to various devices, maintaining both aesthetic integrity and usability.

```css
/* Media queries for responsive design */
@media (max-width: 480px) {
    h1 {
        font-size: 20px;
    }
}
```

This example ensures that the heading remains legible and visually appealing even on smaller devices.

4. Iterative Design Based on User Feedback

Engaging users through testing and feedback is crucial for refining both the aesthetic and functional aspects of the design. This iterative process helps align the design more closely with user needs and preferences.

Conclusion

Successfully balancing aesthetic appeal with usability in UI/UX design enhances user satisfaction and engagement. By employing thoughtful design strategies and continually adapting to user feedback, designers can create interfaces that are both beautiful and functional. This balanced approach is essential for delivering superior user experiences that attract and retain users effectively.

Chapter Two

Color and Visual Psychology

Deeper into Color Interactions and Contrasts

In the field of UI/UX design, understanding color interactions and contrasts transcends aesthetic choices—it fundamentally shapes the user experience. Effective use of color can guide user behavior, direct attention, and significantly influence user interactions with an interface. This discussion delves into the advanced concepts of color theory, focusing on how strategic use of color contrasts and interactions can create intuitive and visually engaging interfaces, supported by practical coding examples.

Understanding Color Interactions

Color interaction involves how different colors influence one another when placed in close proximity. Proper management of these interactions can lead to a visually cohesive and harmonious interface, whereas poor combinations can result in visual tension or discomfort. Key aspects of color interaction include:

- **Contrast**: More than just color difference, contrast includes variations in hue, saturation, and brightness that can help elements stand out or recede.

- **Vibrancy**: The use of vibrant colors can energize a design, affecting the viewer's emotional response, while subdued tones might be used to create a calming atmosphere.

- **Complementary Colors**: Using colors from opposite sides of the color wheel can create dynamic and appealing visuals but requires careful balance to prevent clashes.

- **Analogous Colors**: Colors adjacent on the color wheel work well together and produce a serene and comfortable visual effect.

The Role of Color Psychology in Contrasts

Color psychology is essential in influencing how designs are perceived and interacted with. For example:

- **Red**: Often used to create a sense of urgency or importance, red can draw immediate attention and is effective for warnings or calls to action.

- **Blue**: Commonly associated with stability and professionalism, blue is favored in designs for business and healthcare services due to its calming effect.

Using colors strategically based on their psychological impact can enhance user engagement and direct users effectively through an interface.

Practical Application of Color in UI/UX Design

To successfully implement color interactions and contrasts, designers need to balance aesthetic appeal with functional clarity. Here are some strategies with coding examples:

Optimizing Readability with High Contrast

Using high contrast between text and background is critical for readability, especially for accessibility.

```css
.content {
    color: #000000; /* Black text */
    background-color: #ffffff; /* White background */
}
```

This CSS example ensures optimal contrast, enhancing legibility for a wide range of users.

Using Color to Highlight User Interactions

Employing color to differentiate interactive elements like buttons can guide users to take desired actions.

```css
.primary-action {
    background-color: #0088cc; /* Bright blue */
    color: #ffffff; /* White text */
}

.secondary-action {
    background-color: #cccccc; /* Grey */
    color: #333333; /* Dark grey text */
}
```

This setup uses bright blue to make the primary action button stand out, while secondary actions are more subtly designed.

Setting the Mood with Color Schemes

The choice of colors can set the overall mood of a website or application.

```
.background {
    background-color: #e0ffff; /* Light cyan for a soothing background */
    color: #000000; /* Black for contrast */
}
```

This color scheme uses light cyan to evoke a peaceful atmosphere, suitable for applications focused on relaxation or meditation.

Challenges in Utilizing Color Contrasts

Despite the benefits, color contrasts and interactions come with challenges:

- **Visual Overstimulation**: An overuse of high contrast or vibrant colors can overwhelm users, making it hard to focus on important elements.

- **Cultural Differences**: Colors have varied meanings across cultures, which can alter the perceived message or effectiveness of a design internationally.

Conclusion

Exploring deeper into color interactions and contrasts provides UI/UX designers with the tools to enhance interface design profoundly. By understanding and applying advanced color theory, designers can create interfaces that are not only attractive but also facilitate an intuitive and positive user experience. Careful consideration of color psychology, along with practical implementation strategies, ensures that designs are accessible and effectively guide user behavior.

Emotional Impacts of Color Choices

Color significantly shapes user experience in UI/UX design, not just enhancing the visual appeal but also affecting psychological and behavioral responses. This deep dive into color theory explores how specific hues can manipulate emotions, guide user decisions, and effectively improve user interaction and brand perception.

The Principles of Color Psychology

Color psychology explores how different shades impact feelings and behaviors. Each color triggers specific emotional responses, some universally recognized and others culturally specific. Here are typical responses associated with popular colors:

- **Red**: This vibrant color is associated with energy, action, and urgency. It's often employed to grab attention and prompt immediate reactions, such as in alerts or promotional calls to action.

- **Blue**: Known for its calming effects, blue is used extensively to foster trust and peace, making it ideal for business and healthcare applications.

- **Yellow**: Symbolic of joy and vibrancy, yellow is effective at attracting attention and evoking a sense of optimism. It should be used sparingly to avoid visual overload.

- **Green**: Green connotes balance, health, and renewal, often used by brands promoting environmental and natural themes.

- **Black**: Black suggests sophistication and formality, preferred in luxury branding to communicate elegance and classic style.

- **White**: Indicative of simplicity and purity, white is frequently used to create a clean, uncluttered look, popular in modern design.

Color's Role in User Interaction

Color not only sets the mood but also drives user behavior through strategic placement and contrast within the interface:

```css
.alert-button {
    background-color: #ff4757; /* Vivid Red */
    color: white;
    padding: 10px;
    border-radius: 5px;
}

.proceed-button {
    background-color: #2ed573; /* Soft Green */
    color: white;
    padding: 10px;
    border-radius: 5px;
}
```

In these examples, red is used for alerts to draw immediate attention due to its association with caution, while green suggests safety and is used for actions that users are encouraged to take, facilitating intuitive navigation.

Incorporating Color in Branding

Effective use of color strengthens brand identity and can enhance customer loyalty by making a brand more recognizable and relatable. Consistency in color usage helps cement the emotional ties customers have with a brand, elevating their overall engagement and perception.

Considering Cultural Implications

The interpretation of colors varies globally, which can influence how a design is perceived by different cultures. Designers need to be aware of these variations to ensure their color choices communicate the intended message without cultural missteps.

Conclusion

Understanding and harnessing the emotional impacts of color choices can transform user interactions, making them more engaging and aligned with the desired user behavior. By employing colors thoughtfully, designers can significantly enhance the effectiveness of an interface or brand strategy. Thoughtful color selection, grounded in the principles of color psychology, is essential for delivering compelling user experiences and achieving successful design outcomes, particularly in interfaces where emotional connection and user behavior are critical.

Using Color to Guide User Behavior

In the realm of UI/UX design, the application of color extends far beyond decoration—it profoundly influences how users interact with digital interfaces. This essay explores the nuanced role of color in steering user behaviors, facilitating smooth navigation, and ultimately, enhancing the effectiveness of user interfaces.

The Role of Color in Communication and Design

Color functions as a dynamic communicative tool within design, capable of:

- **Directing User Focus**: Employing vibrant or contrasting colors can draw attention to key interface elements such as alerts and actionable buttons.

- **Influencing Emotions**: Colors trigger specific emotional states; for example, blue can calm, while orange might inspire energy.

- **Boosting Readability and Accessibility**: Adequate color contrast is essential for ensuring that all users, including those with visual impairments, can read and interact with content easily.

Color Strategies for Influencing User Behavior

Color, when used strategically, can effectively lead users toward desired interactions, making experiences both intuitive and rewarding.

Emphasizing Interactive Features

Designing interactive elements with standout colors helps them to catch the user's eye, promoting engagement.

Example in CSS:

```css
.subscribe-button {
    background-color: #FF6347; /* Vivid tomato red */
    color: #FFFFFF; /* White text */
    padding: 12px 26px;
    border-radius: 4px;
    font-weight: bold;
    cursor: pointer;
}
```

Facilitating Navigation Through Color

Using color to differentiate sections within an application can guide users intuitively through a site or app, enhancing user flow and satisfaction.

Example in CSS:

```css
.content-area {
    background-color: #FFFFFF; /* White for main content */
    padding: 20px;
}

.navigation-area {
    background-color: #F0F0F0; /* Light grey for navigation */
    padding: 20px;
}
```

Adjusting Emotional Responses

The application of specific colors can be tailored to evoke the desired emotional response relevant to the app's purpose, whether calming or energizing.

Example in CSS:

```css
.meditation-app {
    background-color: #AED6F1; /* Light blue for a calming effect */
    color: #154360; /* Deep blue for text */
}

.fitness-app {
    background-color: #FF4500; /* Orange-red for energy */
    color: #FFFFFF;
}
```

Navigating the Challenges of Color Usage

While color is a potent tool in design, its use is not without challenges:

- **Avoiding Overstimulation**: An excess of bright or clashing colors can create a jarring experience, detracting from usability.

- **Cultural Sensitivity**: The meaning of colors varies significantly across cultures, potentially altering the intended impact of a design internationally.

Conclusion

The strategic use of color in UI/UX design not only beautifies but serves as a critical guide in user behavior and interface navigation. By understanding and implementing color psychology, designers can create more engaging, functional, and accessible interfaces. Thoughtful color usage, supported by precise coding examples, enhances the digital environment, making it more appealing and effective for a diverse user base.

Chapter Three

Sophisticated Typography

Advanced Typography and Readability

In the digital realm, advanced typography is critical for optimizing the design and functionality of interfaces, profoundly impacting user comprehension and interaction. This detailed overview focuses on the nuanced application of typography that promotes readability and facilitates smoother navigation across user interfaces.

Role of Typography in UI/UX Design

Effective typography transcends the mere selection of fonts; it involves the strategic arrangement and application of type to maximize legibility and aesthetic value. Key elements of typography that significantly influence readability include:

Font Selection

The type of font used is pivotal in affecting text clarity. Serif fonts, often preferred in print, are useful in digital contexts at larger sizes for headings due to their formal appearance. Sans-serif fonts, noted for their straightforward and clean appearance, are typically favored for body text in digital formats because they render more cleanly on diverse screen types.

Example in CSS:

```css
.content-text {
    font-family: 'Roboto', sans-serif; /* Renowned for its clarity and versatility */
    font-size: 16px; /* Optimal for reading on digital screens */
}
```

Arrangement of Text

How text is structured—including the choice of line length, alignment, and spacing between lines—greatly affects readability. Properly arranged text aids in maintaining user focus and enhancing content absorption.

Example in CSS:

```css
.article-content {
    max-width: 680px; /* Limits line length to improve readability */
    text-align: left; /* Maintains a consistent flow for text */
    line-height: 1.8; /* Provides ample line spacing for clarity */
    margin-bottom: 32px; /* Ensures proper separation for distinct paragraphs */
}
```

Typography Spacing Techniques

Kerning, tracking, and leading are essential typographic adjustments that contribute to a balanced and readable text presentation. These adjustments help in making the text not just readable but visually appealing.

Example in CSS:

```css
.header-text {
    letter-spacing: 0.1px; /* Subtly adjusts spacing between characters in headings */
    line-height: 1.4; /* Optimal line height for header visibility */
}
```

Enhancing Accessibility with Typography

Ensuring typography is accessible to all users, including those with disabilities, is a crucial aspect of UI design. It involves using fonts that are distinguishable and ensuring there is high contrast between the text and its background.

Example in CSS:

```css
.readable-design {
    font-family: 'Verdana', sans-serif; /* Chosen for its clear, spacious design */
    color: #333333; /* High contrast for better readability */
    background-color: #FFFFFF; /* Provides a bright contrast to the text color */
}
```

Responsive Typography

Adapting typography for different devices ensures that text is equally legible and visually consistent no matter the screen size.

Example in CSS:

```css
@media (max-width: 480px) {
    .content-text {
        font-size: 14px; /* Smaller font size for mobile devices to maintain legibility */
    }
}
```

Emotional and Aesthetic Contributions of Typography

Typography also affects the emotional and atmospheric aspects of a digital product. It can reflect a brand's identity and influence the overall mood of the interface.

Conclusion

Advanced typography is a cornerstone in crafting effective digital interfaces. It plays an integral role in enhancing readability, ensuring accessibility, and contributing to the overall user experience. Through careful planning and implementation of typographic principles, designers can significantly improve how content is perceived and engaged with, leading to a more user-friendly and appealing digital environment.

Microtypography: Details that Matter

Microtypography examines the minute, often overlooked elements of typography that significantly influence text clarity, engagement, and aesthetic quality. It includes precise adjustments to kerning, tracking, ligatures, and punctuation, all of which are essential for crafting superior textual presentations in both print and digital media.

The Critical Role of Microtypography

Microtypography focuses on the fine details within type settings that, while small, play a major role in the legibility and overall presentation of text.

Kerning

Kerning adjusts the spaces between specific character pairs to prevent unsightly gaps and create a visually uniform appearance. This adjustment is vital for enhancing the text's readability and aesthetic appeal.

Example in CSS:

```css
.main-title {
    font-family: 'Helvetica', sans-serif;
    font-size: 26px;
    letter-spacing: -0.2px; /* Optimizes kerning for visual harmony */
}
```

Tracking

Tracking involves adjusting the spacing across large blocks of text to modify its density and texture, improving readability and visual comfort, especially in digital settings where display sizes vary.

Example in CSS:

```css
.body-content {
    font-family: 'Roboto', sans-serif;
    letter-spacing: 0.12px; /* Slightly expands spacing for better readability */
}
```

Ligatures

Ligatures combine two or more letters into a single glyph, enhancing the flow and appearance of text. They are especially useful in high-quality typefaces to prevent letter clashing and improve text continuity.

Example in CSS:

```css
.content {
    font-family: 'Adobe Garamond Pro', serif;
    font-feature-settings: "liga" 1; /* Activates ligatures for aesthetic improvement */
}
```

Punctuation and Special Characters

Proper use of punctuation marks and special characters is crucial for clarity and accuracy in textual communication. Microtypography ensures these characters are used correctly, enhancing the professional quality of the text.

Example in CSS:

```css
.narrative {
    quotes: "“" "”" "‘" "’"; /* Correctly uses curly quotes for dialogue */
    font-size: 16px;
    font-style: italic;
    margin: 10px 0;
}
```

Enhancing User Experience Through Microtypography

Attention to microtypographical details can dramatically improve how users interact with text by making it more accessible and enjoyable to read. These small adjustments signal a high level of care in design, contributing to the content's credibility and the user's trust.

Conclusion

Although microtypography concerns subtle aspects of typography, its impact on the effectiveness of communication and design is immense. By meticulously managing kerning, tracking, ligatures, and punctuation, designers can greatly enhance text presentation. This not only aids in readability but also enriches the visual appeal, making microtypography an indispensable element in sophisticated design practices.

Using Typography to Enhance UX

In the field of user interface (UI) design, effective typography transcends mere visual decoration, acting as a key enhancer of user experience (UX). It organizes and prioritizes information while setting an emotional tone, thereby guiding users through digital interactions with ease. This discussion will articulate how thoughtful typography can modify user behavior, improve interface usability, and amplify brand identity.

Emotional Impact of Typography

The typeface selected can profoundly impact user emotions and perceptions. Serif fonts may communicate a sense of trust and tradition, suitable for sectors like banking, while sans-serif fonts, often sleek and modern, might be favored by technology companies aiming to project efficiency and innovation.

The implementation of typography extends its influence beyond aesthetic appeal to affect user interaction dynamics. Incorrectly chosen typography can lead to user disengagement, reduced accessibility, and even abandonment of the interface. On the other hand, skillfully chosen and applied typography enhances readability, fosters user engagement, and boosts overall satisfaction with the digital experience.

Typography in User Interface Elements

The role of typography is critical when designing actionable UI elements like buttons and menus. It impacts how users perceive and interact with these elements. For instance, effective typography can transform a simple call-to-action button into a compelling invitation for user engagement.

41

Here's a CSS snippet to demonstrate optimized typography for a button:

```css
.button {
    background-color: #0066ff; /* Striking blue to catch the eye */
    color: white; /* Stark contrast for clear visibility */
    font-family: Arial, sans-serif; /* Direct and unambiguous font */
    font-size: 16px; /* Optimized size for legibility */
    font-weight: bold; /* Bold for emphasis */
    padding: 12px 24px; /* Generous padding to facilitate clicking */
    border-radius: 8px; /* Gentle curves for a modern feel */
    text-transform: uppercase; /* Uppercase for distinctiveness */
    box-shadow: 0 4px 8px rgba(0,0,0,0.1); /* Subtle shadow for depth */
}
```

This code enhances the button's visual and functional attributes, making it immediately more engaging and easier to use with its clear, readable typography.

Typography and Brand Identity

Typography is a powerful tool for reinforcing brand identity and ensuring visual coherence across user interfaces. It delivers the brand's voice and ethos—whether that communicates luxury, sophistication, or approachability. Consistent typography aids in building brand recognition and trust.

Maintaining typographic consistency, especially across various platforms and devices, is crucial and can be effectively managed through responsive design practices:

```css
html {
  font-size: 100%; /* Base size on desktop */
}

@media (max-width: 768px) {
  html {
    font-size: 90%; /* Adjust for tablet screens */
  }
}

@media (max-width: 480px) {
  html {
    font-size: 80%; /* Reduce for mobile screens */
  }
}
```

These CSS media queries help in adapting typography to different screen sizes, ensuring that it remains legible and consistent, thus preserving the user experience and brand integrity across devices.

Conclusion

Typography is more than just a design choice; it is a strategic tool crucial for the functionality and effectiveness of UI/UX design. By strategically utilizing typography, designers can direct user behavior, improve usability, and ensure cohesive brand representation across all digital platforms. Typography should be seen as an essential component of the design process, integral to crafting successful user interfaces.

Chapter Four

Designing for Navigation Efficiency

Advanced Navigation Schemes

Navigational efficiency is pivotal in crafting a user interface (UI) that offers an optimal user experience (UX). As digital platforms grow in complexity, incorporating sophisticated navigation systems becomes crucial. These systems are designed to facilitate ease of navigation and improve the accessibility of extensive information without overwhelming the user. This article will explore various advanced navigation strategies that streamline user interactions and boost functional efficiency across diverse digital platforms.

Importance of Advanced Navigation

Advanced navigation systems are tailored to manage and simplify complex information architectures, enhancing user accessibility and minimizing cognitive load. These systems are particularly valuable in applications with intricate content structures or extensive data. Effective navigation employs a mix of dynamic elements, layout optimizations, and predictive technologies to lead users through a digital product seamlessly.

Mega Menus in Action

Mega menus are a favored navigation tool in environments like large-scale e-commerce sites or expansive enterprise applications. They present a wide array of options in an organized manner by grouping related topics within a single, expansive panel. This arrangement keeps the interface uncluttered and provides users with a clear overview of available content categories at a glance.

Here is an example of CSS code for a basic mega menu:

```css
.nav-menu {
  display: flex;
  justify-content: space-between;
  list-style-type: none;
}
.mega-menu {
  position: absolute;
  width: 100%;
  display: none;
  box-shadow: 0px 8px 16px 0px rgba(0,0,0,0.2);
  z-index: 1;
}
.nav-menu li:hover .mega-menu {
  display: block;
}
.mega-menu-content {
  display: flex;
  flex-direction: row;
  padding: 20px;
  background-color: white;
}
.mega-menu-section {
  margin-right: 40px;
}
```

This CSS setup outlines the structure for a mega menu, which expands to show different sections filled with navigational links or content summaries when a user hovers over a menu item.

Hidden Menus for Minimalist Design

Hidden menus, often symbolized by a 'hamburger' icon, are another popular advanced navigation choice. They are particularly useful in designs aiming for a minimalist look or in mobile-responsive settings. The navigation options are typically hidden and only become visible upon user interaction.

Below is a straightforward implementation of a responsive hamburger menu using HTML, CSS, and JavaScript:

```
<!DOCTYPE html>
<html>
<head>
<style>
  .menu {
    width: 100%;
    background: #333;
    overflow: auto;
  }
  .menu-content {
    display: none;
    padding: 15px;
    background: white;
    color: black;
  }
  .menu-icon {
    padding: 15px;
    background: #333;
    color: white;
    cursor: pointer;
  }
</style>
</head>
<body>
```

```
<div class="menu">
  <div class="menu-icon" onclick="toggleMenu()">≡ Menu</div>
  <div class="menu-content">
    <a href="#">Home</a>
    <a href="#">About</a>
    <a href="#">Services</a>
    <a href="#">Contact</a>
  </div>
</div>

<script>
function toggleMenu() {
  var x = document.getElementById("menuContent");
  if (x.style.display === "block") {
    x.style.display = "none";
  } else {
    x.style.display = "block";
  }
}
</script>

</body>
</html>
```

Adaptive Navigation Driven by User Interaction

Adaptive or dynamic navigation schemes customize the navigation experience based on user behavior and predictive analysis, utilizing AI and machine learning. These systems are increasingly utilized in platforms that adapt to user preferences, such as personalized e-commerce sites or adaptive educational technologies.

While the backend implementation of such adaptive systems might be complex, involving extensive use of data analytics, the frontend result is a highly tailored user experience that significantly enhances interaction ease and personal relevance.

Conclusion

In the evolving landscape of digital UI/UX design, advanced navigation schemes play a crucial role in enhancing user interaction and accessibility. Whether through the use of mega menus, hidden menus, or intelligent, adaptive systems, these advanced strategies ensure that navigating complex digital environments is intuitive and efficient for all users. As technologies advance, navigation strategies will continue to develop, always with the aim of improving the coherence and intuitiveness of user interactions.

Implementing Mega Menus and Hidden Menus

Navigational elements like mega menus and hidden menus are essential tools in the arsenal of UI/UX designers, particularly for sites with extensive content arrays. These elements provide structured and intuitive access to information, critical for improving the user interface of large-scale digital properties. This article explores the design specifics and technical aspects of integrating mega menus and hidden menus, which are pivotal for facilitating effective user navigation in complex web environments.

Implementing Mega Menus

Mega menus offer a way to display extensive navigation links grouped under broad headings in a single, overarching panel. This method is particularly useful for sites that need to present multiple options across categories, such as large retail sites or corporate portals. Mega menus allow users to overview and access a wide range of content quickly.

Technical Details:

Setting up a mega menu typically involves using HTML, CSS, and JavaScript. Here's an example illustrating how to implement a responsive mega menu effectively:

```html
<!-- HTML for mega menu setup -->
<nav class="navbar">
  <ul class="nav-links">
    <li class="nav-item" onmouseover="toggleVisibility('mega-menu-1')">Products
      <div class="mega-menu" id="mega-menu-1">
        <!-- Sections within mega menu -->
        <div class="menu-column">
          <h4>Category 1</h4>
          <a href="#">Item 1</a>
          <a href="#">Item 2</a>
          <a href="#">Item 3</a>
        </div>
        <div class="menu-column">
          <h4>Category 2</h4>
          <a href="#">Item 1</a>
          <a href="#">Item 2</a>
          <a href="#">Item 3</a>
        </div>
      </div>
    </li>
    <!-- Additional nav-items -->
  </ul>
</nav>
```

```css
/* CSS for mega menu appearance */
.navbar .nav-links .nav-item .mega-menu {
  display: none;
  position: absolute;
  background-color: #fff;
  width: 100%;
  box-shadow: 0 8px 16px rgba(0,0,0,0.2);
}

.navbar .nav-links .nav-item:hover .mega-menu {
  display: block;
}
```

```javascript
// JavaScript to manage menu visibility
function toggleVisibility(id) {
  var element = document.getElementById(id);
  if (element.style.display === 'none') {
    element.style.display = 'block';
  } else {
    element.style.display = 'none';
  }
}
```

This snippet demonstrates how hovering over a menu item displays a well-organized panel that groups navigation links effectively.

Implementing Hidden Menus

Hidden menus, or "hamburger menus," are icons used extensively in mobile UI design to conserve space while providing necessary navigation capabilities. This type of menu keeps the interface clean and uncluttered, with navigation options that are accessible via user interaction.

Technical Details:

Creating a hidden menu involves HTML for structure, CSS for styling, and JavaScript for functionality. Below is a basic example:

```html
<!-- HTML for hidden menu -->
<div class="menu-icon" onclick="toggleMenu()">☰</div>
<div class="hidden-menu" id="hidden-menu">
  <a href="#">Home</a>
  <a href="#">About</a>
  <a href="#">Services</a>
  <a href="#">Contact</a>
</div>
```

```css
/* CSS for the hidden menu styling */
.hidden-menu {
  display: none;
  background-color: #333;
  color: white;
  width: 100%;
}

.menu-icon {
  cursor: pointer;
}
```

```javascript
// JavaScript to control menu display
function toggleMenu() {
  var menu = document.getElementById('hidden-menu');
  if (menu.style.display === 'none') {
    menu.style.display = 'block';
  } else {
    menu.style.display = 'none';
  }
}
```

This code creates a collapsible menu that users can reveal and conceal with a click, enhancing the mobile experience by maximizing the usable screen area.

Conclusion

Mega menus and hidden menus are critical components in the design of modern websites, especially those requiring a sophisticated approach to navigation due to their vast content. When implemented properly, these navigational elements not only streamline access to information but also significantly enhance the aesthetic and functional quality of the site, ensuring a superior user experience across various platforms and devices.

Customizing Navigation for Complex Sites

For websites that house a wealth of information and diverse functionalities, navigation is not just a component—it's a critical infrastructure that guides every user interaction. Effective navigation design requires a combination of in-depth user insights and robust technical strategies. This article examines the best practices for designing navigation that meets the complexities of sophisticated websites, incorporating practical code examples for clarity.

Gathering User Insights

A tailored navigation system starts with a deep dive into user behavior. Employing methods such as user personas, journey mapping, and targeted usability testing can unveil how users prefer to navigate, what information they seek, and the common issues they encounter. These insights directly inform the navigation structure, making it more aligned with user needs and expectations.

Structuring Information Architecture

Effective information architecture (IA) is crucial for laying out content in an organized and intuitive manner. For complex sites, this means establishing a clear hierarchy that breaks down information from general to specific. Here's a straightforward depiction of a sitemap that could help visualize the IA:

```
Home
|- Products
|  |- Product Category 1
|      |- Subcategory A
|      |- Subcategory B
|  |- Product Category 2
|      |- Subcategory C
|      |- Subcategory D
|- Services
|  |- Service 1
|  |- Service 2
|- About Us
|- Contact
```

This layout assists in designing a navigational framework that users can understand and navigate without confusion.

Dynamic Navigation Components

To enhance the user interface on complex sites, dynamic navigation components like mega menus and faceted search are invaluable. These tools allow users to access deep content quickly and effortlessly. For example, a mega menu can provide immediate access to multiple layers of the site directly from the main navigation bar.

Below is a basic implementation of a mega menu using HTML and CSS:

```html
<!-- HTML for Mega Menu -->
<div class="mega-menu">
  <div class="column">
    <h4>Category 1</h4>
    <a href="#">Link 1</a>
    <a href="#">Link 2</a>
    <a href="#">Link 3</a>
  </div>
  <div class="column">
    <h4>Category 2</h4>
    <a href="#">Link 4</a>
    <a href="#">Link 5</a>
    <a href="#">Link 6</a>
  </div>
</div>
```

```css
/* CSS for Mega Menu */
.mega-menu {
  display: none;
  position: absolute;
  background-color: white;
  box-shadow: 0px 5px 15px rgba(0,0,0,0.2);
  width: 100%;
}
.mega-menu .column {
  float: left;
  width: 25%;
  padding: 10px;
}
.mega-menu:hover {
  display: block;
}
```

Responsive Navigation Solutions

Responsive navigation ensures that a site's navigation system works seamlessly across different devices. For smaller screens, such as those on mobile devices, implementing a collapsible menu (often displayed as a hamburger icon) optimizes space and maintains usability.

Here's a JavaScript function to handle a responsive navigation menu:

```javascript
function toggleMenu() {
  var x = document.getElementById("myTopnav");
  if (x.className === "topnav") {
    x.className += " responsive";
  } else {
    x.className = "topnav";
  }
}
```

Navigation Accessibility

Accessibility is paramount in navigation design. Ensuring that all navigation elements are accessible through keyboard and assistive devices, implementing ARIA roles, and maintaining high contrast are all necessary to make navigation user-friendly for all visitors.

```html
<!-- Accessible navigation example -->
<a href="#" aria-label="Learn more about product 1" role="button">Product 1</a>
```

Conclusion

Designing navigation for complex sites demands a strategic approach that combines user-centric insights, structured information architecture, and advanced technical implementations. By applying these principles, developers and designers can create navigation systems that not only meet the demands of complex websites but also enhance the overall user experience, making it smoother and more intuitive.

Chapter Five

Iconography and Symbolism

Creating Custom Icons

Custom icons are vital elements in UI/UX design, enhancing both the functionality and aesthetic appeal of digital interfaces. They simplify user interactions and contribute to a cohesive visual style that supports the brand's identity. This article outlines the process for designing and implementing effective custom icons, from initial sketches to deployment.

The Importance of Icons in User Interfaces

Icons act as intuitive cues that facilitate quicker and easier navigation through digital products, effectively reducing the time users spend deciphering functionality. They streamline interfaces by replacing text, making operations visually comprehensible and swift.

Fundamental Design Guidelines for Custom Icons

Developing custom icons requires adherence to several important design guidelines:

- **Clarity and Visibility**: Icons should immediately convey their function and be understandable at a glance, without any need for contemplation.

- **Consistency in Style**: To ensure the interface remains harmonious, all icons should follow a uniform design approach in terms of line width, color scheme, and visual proportions.

- **Responsive and Scalable**: Design icons to be legible across all device types and sizes, from tiny mobile screens to large desktop displays.

The initial design phase typically involves rough sketches, either on paper or using digital tools such as Adobe Illustrator for creating scalable vector images.

Technical Steps for Icon Creation

The creation of custom icons includes several technical phases:

1. **Drafting Concepts**: Begin with hand-drawn concepts or basic digital drafts to capture creative ideas.

2. **Vectorization**: Convert these drafts into polished vectors, using software that allows for fine-tuning and easy adjustments.

3. **Digital Optimization**: Prepare icons for use across various platforms by optimizing for size and resolution to ensure they load efficiently and display crisply.

For instance, here's how you might code a simple SVG for a custom icon:

```
<svg height="100" width="100">
  <rect x="25" y="25" width="50" height="50" fill="purple"/>
</svg>
```

This SVG code generates a straightforward square icon, suitable for multiple uses due to its vector nature.

Strategies for Icon Integration

Effective integration of icons into digital projects can be achieved through several methods:

- **SVGs in Web Content**: Directly embedding SVG files into HTML ensures that icons scale perfectly and remain sharp across all resolutions.

- **CSS Backgrounds**: Using icons as CSS backgrounds for web elements can streamline design coherence and simplify icon management.

- **Icon Font Creation**: Compiling icons into a custom font allows for easy styling and uniformity across a website or application.

Here's a CSS example for using an icon as a background image:

```css
.icon-style {
  width: 60px;
  height: 60px;
  background-image: url('path/to/your-icon.svg');
  background-repeat: no-repeat;
  background-size: contain;
}
```

This CSS configuration sets the icon as a scalable background, ensuring it fits well within the designated space.

Icon Accessibility Considerations

It's essential that icons are accessible to all users, including those with visual impairments. This means incorporating textual descriptions and ensuring icons are perceivable by assistive technologies.

```
<button aria-label="Expand menu">
  <svg viewBox="0 0 24 24">
    <path d="M3,6h18M3,12h18M3,18h18" stroke="black" stroke-width="2"/>
  </svg>
</button>
```

This button with a menu icon uses an aria-label to describe its function, making it accessible to users utilizing screen readers.

Conclusion

The thoughtful design and implementation of custom icons are crucial for creating effective and engaging user interfaces. By focusing on simplicity, consistency, and scalability, and ensuring icons are accessible, designers can elevate the user experience, providing not only visual enhancement but also functional improvement in navigating digital environments. Icons are powerful tools in the UI/UX toolkit, offering a blend of aesthetic appeal and practical utility.

Symbolism in UI Design

Symbolism is a critical component in the field of user interface (UI) design, serving as a conduit for conveying intricate messages and emotions efficiently. Utilizing symbolic imagery, designers can increase user engagement, improve navigation, and communicate core brand values succinctly. This article examines the role of symbolism in UI design, discusses its influence on user perception and behavior, and outlines methods for integrating effective symbols into digital interfaces.

Importance of Symbolism in Digital Interfaces

Symbols are integral to how information is communicated universally. They enable quick recognition and understanding, facilitating a smoother user interaction with digital platforms. In UI design, thoughtfully chosen symbols can transcend language barriers, making applications more accessible and intuitive to a global audience.

Emotional Impact and Cultural Sensitivity

The choice of symbols can deeply affect the emotional response of users. For instance, a heart symbol commonly represents affection and is widely used across various platforms to denote approval or favor (e.g., liking a post on social media). However, cultural sensitivity is crucial; symbols must be selected and used with an understanding of their cultural implications to avoid misinterpretations that could detract from the user experience.

Guidelines for Using Symbols in UI Design

When integrating symbols into a UI, designers should consider:

- **Immediate Recognizability**: Symbols should be instantly clear to users, avoiding any potential confusion.

- **Design Cohesion**: Maintain a consistent visual style for all symbols within the application to support a unified brand identity.

- **Context and Appropriateness**: Ensure that symbols used are appropriate for their specific context, aiding rather than complicating the user's understanding.

Techniques for Integrating Symbols

Effective symbol integration in UI design can be achieved through various applications:

1. **Enhanced Navigation**: Using symbols to denote different sections or functionalities, such as a house for 'home' or a gear for 'settings', simplifies the interface and aids memory recall.

2. **Actionable Elements**: Symbols are commonly employed in interactive elements like buttons to prompt user actions, such as using a plus sign for 'add' or a trash can for 'delete'.

3. **Status Indicators**: Symbols provide feedback on actions, such as a spinner for loading or a checkmark for completion.

Utilizing SVG for Precision and Scalability

Scalable Vector Graphics (SVG) are particularly suited for implementing symbols in digital designs. SVGs offer clarity regardless of screen size, maintaining the quality and effectiveness of the symbolism across different devices. Here is an SVG implementation example:

```
<svg height="50" width="50">
  <circle cx="25" cy="25" r="20" stroke="black" stroke-width="3" fill="red" />
</svg>
```

This SVG code snippet creates a basic red circle, a versatile symbol that can be adapted for various uses such as a recording indicator or as a graphical element in games.

Real-World Application: A Case Example

Consider a navigation app that uses common symbols like an arrow for direction, a magnifying glass for search, and a house for home. Consistently using these symbols throughout the app not only reinforces user learning but also supports quick navigation, enhancing the overall user experience.

Challenges in Symbol Usage

The primary challenge in using symbols is ensuring they are understood universally. What may be clear in one culture can be ambiguous or even offensive in another. Conducting extensive user testing with diverse groups can help identify potential issues with symbolism, ensuring that symbols are both effective and culturally appropriate.

Conclusion

Symbolism in UI design is an essential strategy for creating interfaces that are both aesthetically pleasing and functionally superior. Symbols streamline interactions, reinforce brand identity, and convey complex information efficiently. By carefully selecting and implementing appropriate symbols, and ensuring they are scalable and accessible, designers can significantly enhance the usability and appeal of their digital products.

Icons for Global Audiences

In the digital world, icons are indispensable tools for enhancing user interfaces that need to communicate effectively with an international audience. These visual elements serve as quick, intuitive guides that help users from diverse linguistic and cultural backgrounds navigate software and websites more easily. This article explores the essentials of crafting icons that appeal globally, discussing cultural sensitivity, the pursuit of simplicity, and integration tactics.

The Role of Icons in Cross-Cultural Design

Icons are key in delivering information visually, circumventing language barriers, and speeding up user interactions. While some icons, like a magnifying glass for search, are nearly universal, assumptions about the global recognition of certain icons can lead to misunderstandings. It's crucial for designers to recognize that icons may not be interpreted similarly across all cultures.

Culturally Attuned Icon Design

Creating icons that are embraced on a global scale involves recognizing and respecting cultural diversity in symbolism. An icon that is viewed positively in one culture might be neutral or even negative in another. Conducting comprehensive cultural research and testing icons in diverse markets are essential steps to ensure icons are appropriate and effective worldwide.

Strategies for Crafting Effective Global Icons

Designing icons that resonate with users around the world involves several strategic considerations:

1. **Extensive Cultural Research**: Engaging with international users to understand their perspectives can help identify which icons work and which do not.

2. **Design for Simplicity**: Simplifying icons to their basic elements helps reduce the potential for cultural misinterpretation. Abstract icons generally achieve better universality.

3. **Consistency is Key**: Maintain consistent visual properties across all icons used in an application to ensure a seamless user experience.

4. **Ensure Accessibility**: Icons should be easily identifiable for all users, including those with visual impairments, by considering factors like size, color contrast, and textual descriptions for assistive technologies.

Example: Redesigning the 'Save' Icon for Broad Appeal

The challenge of redesigning a 'save' icon exemplifies the need for modern symbols. The traditional floppy disk may no longer be recognizable to younger or less tech-experienced users globally. A more contemporary approach could be an icon depicting a cloud with a downward arrow, symbolizing saving data to cloud storage.

Here's how you might code such an icon using SVG:

```
<svg xmlns="http://www.w3.org/2000/svg" height="24" width="24" fill="none" stroke
    ="currentColor" stroke-width="2">
  <path d="M6 6L18 18M6 18L18 6" stroke="black" stroke-width="2" fill="none"/>
</svg>
```

This SVG demonstrates a straightforward, stylized icon that could be universally understood as an action to 'save' or 'secure' data.

Navigating Challenges in Icon Design for Global Audiences

Creating universally understood icons is challenging because cultural perceptions vary widely. Icons that are entirely clear in one cultural context may be ambiguous or misleading in another. Ongoing adaptation based on user feedback and potential localization of icons are crucial for meeting the needs of specific markets.

Conclusion

Crafting icons for a global audience requires a delicate balance between universal design and local cultural nuances. By focusing on simple, consistent, and culturally aware designs, and by rigorously testing these icons with diverse user groups, designers can develop effective visual tools that enhance the functionality and appeal of digital interfaces across the world. As digital interfaces become more globally accessible, the careful design of icons will continue to play a critical role in ensuring successful and meaningful user interactions.

Chapter Six

Interactive Elements and Animation

Transitions and Micro-interactions

Transitions and micro-interactions are indispensable elements within UI design, crucial for enhancing the interactive experience of digital applications. They provide smooth visual narratives and immediate feedback to user inputs, which helps in making user interfaces intuitive and engaging. This article highlights the significance of these elements, illustrates their impact on the user experience, and details methods for their implementation.

The Role of Transitions and Micro-interactions

Transitions involve the movement or animation between UI states, which can include page animations or dynamic effects within components. Micro-interactions are brief animations that respond to user actions, such as a color change on a button when clicked or a subtle bounce on an icon. These elements are fundamental for several reasons:

1. **Boosting User Engagement**: Adding depth to interactions that keeps users interested and involved.

2. **Visual Feedback**: Offering instant feedback on the user's actions to assure them that the system is reactive.

3. **Guiding User Actions**: Highlighting elements or changes on the UI that guide users through their tasks.

4. **Simplifying Navigation**: Making complex interfaces more approachable by visually breaking down sequences of user actions.

Implementing Transitions and Micro-interactions

Effective deployment of transitions and micro-interactions can significantly enhance user interfaces in various ways:

- **Through User Journeys**: Smooth transitions can indicate progression or hierarchy within the application, aiding in user orientation.

- **Feedback and Interaction**: Implementing micro-interactions for elements like buttons or sliders to show their state or action, enriching the tactile feel of the UI.

- **Indicators of Activity**: Using animations to show progress or loading states helps in setting the right expectations about processing times.

- **Enhanced Data Engagement**: Animations can draw attention to specific pieces of data, helping with their interpretation and engagement.

Using CSS for Fluid Transitions

CSS provides a powerful means to implement graceful transitions that improve the flow of interactions. Here's how to enhance a UI button with CSS transitions:

```css
.button {
  background-color: #0084FF;
  color: white;
  padding: 12px 24px;
  border-radius: 4px;
  transition: background-color 0.25s ease-in-out;
}

.button:hover {
  background-color: #0056CC;
}
```

This snippet ensures that the button's background color smoothly transitions upon hovering, signaling interactivity visually.

Complex Micro-interactions with JavaScript

JavaScript can be employed for more complex behaviors in micro-interactions, such as a switch that changes its state interactively:

html

```html
<button id="toggleBtn" onclick="toggleButton()">
  <span class="icon">&#9658;</span> Start
</button>
```

css

```css
button {
  padding: 10px;
  font-size: 16px;
  cursor: pointer;
}
.icon {
  margin-right: 10px;
}
```

javascript

```javascript
function toggleButton() {
  var btn = document.getElementById('toggleBtn');
  var icon = btn.querySelector('.icon');
  if (btn.innerText.includes('Start')) {
    icon.innerHTML = '&#10074;&#10074;'; // Change to pause icon
    btn.innerText = ' Pause';
  } else {
    icon.innerHTML = '&#9658;'; // Change back to start icon
    btn.innerText = ' Start';
  }
}
```

This code toggles the button's icon and label between "Start" and "Pause", offering not just visual but also functional feedback to the user.

Design Considerations

While designing transitions and micro-interactions, it's crucial not to overdo them. Excessive use can lead to distraction and decrease overall usability. It's essential to maintain balance, ensuring that each animation adds value to the user experience without overshadowing the core functionality of the application.

Conclusion

Incorporating well-thought-out transitions and micro-interactions into UI design not only improves the aesthetics of digital products but also their usability and effectiveness. By carefully planning and implementing these elements, designers can provide users with fluid, intuitive, and satisfying interactions. As UI design evolves, the nuanced use of these dynamic elements will continue to be integral to creating superior user experiences.

Timing and Choreography of Elements

Timing and choreography are integral to the discipline of UI design, profoundly impacting the user experience by enhancing the interactive dynamics of an interface. These design strategies involve the deliberate arrangement and timing of visual elements to create seamless, engaging user interactions. This article discusses the importance of mastering timing and choreography, outlines key principles, and demonstrates how to apply these concepts effectively through code examples.

The Significance of Timing and Choreography

In UI design, timing refers to the control over the speed and delay of transitions and animations. Choreography relates to the sequence and coordination of these animations to ensure they function harmoniously. Proper execution of these elements facilitates a more intuitive and appealing interface by guiding user interactions and enhancing the visual narrative.

Key Principles of Effective Timing

1. **Uniformity**: Keeping animation speeds and delays consistent across the UI helps maintain a smooth user experience and avoids disorienting transitions.

2. **Optimal Speed**: Animations should be quick enough to keep up with user expectations yet slow enough to be appreciated. Durations typically range from 200 to 500 milliseconds.

3. **Natural Movement**: Utilizing easing functions can make transitions appear more fluid and realistic, avoiding the mechanical feel of linear animations.

Key Principles of Effective Choreography

1. **Intentional Movement**: Animations should serve a definite purpose, such as directing attention or enhancing the storytelling within the UI.

2. **Directional Focus**: Strategic animations can effectively lead the user's gaze to important information or action areas.

3. **Unified Approach**: Ensuring that all animated elements work together in a cohesive manner enhances the overall experience and prevents visual clutter.

Advantages of Well-Implemented Timing and Choreography

- **Boosted Engagement**: Engaging animations can captivate users, making even routine interactions interesting and reducing perceived wait times.

- **Enhanced Navigation**: Thoughtfully choreographed movements can help users navigate the interface more naturally, clarifying relationships between different elements.

- **Elevated Design Aesthetics**: Smooth and consistent animations contribute to a polished look, improving the overall perception of the application.

Practical Example: Implementing CSS and JavaScript

To demonstrate the application of these principles, consider the example of animating a set of progress bars that fill up sequentially:

HTML Structure:

```html
<div class="progress-bar"></div>
<div class="progress-bar"></div>
<div class="progress-bar"></div>
```

CSS for Animation:

```css
.progress-bar {
  width: 0%;
  height: 20px;
  background-color: #6789CA;
  margin-top: 5px;
  animation: fill 2s ease-in-out infinite;
}

@keyframes fill {
  0%, 100% {
    width: 0%;
  }
  50% {
    width: 100%;
  }
}
```

JavaScript for Choreography:

```javascript
const progressBars = document.querySelectorAll('.progress-bar');
progressBars.forEach((bar, index) => {
  // Stagger the animation start times
  bar.style.animationDelay = `${index * 0.5}s`;
});
```

In this setup, each progress bar fills and empties in turn, creating a dynamic wave effect. The staggered start times (controlled by JavaScript) and the ease-in-out animation (defined in CSS) work together to produce a visually appealing sequence.

Challenges in Design

Implementing timing and choreography requires careful consideration to balance visual appeal with usability. Excessive or poorly timed animations can be distracting and may complicate the user experience rather than enrich it. Designers must strive to find a balance that enhances interactivity without overwhelming users.

Conclusion

Mastering the timing and choreography of elements within UI design is crucial for creating compelling and functional interfaces. These strategies, when applied judiciously, can significantly enhance the aesthetics and usability of digital products, leading to a more enjoyable and engaging user experience. As designers continue to innovate, the thoughtful integration of these dynamic elements will remain essential to the evolution of UI design.

Animation for Feedback and Engagement

In user interface (UI) design, animations enrich the interaction between users and digital products, serving dual purposes: providing feedback and fostering engagement. Properly designed animations clarify the results of user actions and make the interaction process more engaging, thus enhancing the overall user experience. This article explores how animations can be strategically used for feedback and engagement in UI design, discusses the principles behind them, and offers practical coding examples for effective implementation.

The Functional Importance of Animation in UI Feedback

Animations in UI design are essential for indicating system responses to user interactions. This visual communication is crucial as it helps prevent user errors and increases the interface's responsiveness.

Core Functions of Feedback Animation:

- **Acknowledgment**: Animations that acknowledge user actions, like an animated tick after a form submission, reassure users that their input has been successfully received.

- **Progress Tracking**: They can visually depict the progress of a task, using elements like animated progress bars or spinning wheels.

- **Error Indication**: Highlighting mistakes through animations, such as a shake effect on a text field with an invalid entry, promptly notifies users of errors.

Enhancing User Engagement Through Animation

Animations also play a vital role in engaging users by making the experience more dynamic and visually stimulating.

Benefits of Engagement-Oriented Animation:

- **Increased Aesthetic Value**: Subtle animations can significantly enhance the visual appeal of an application, making it more attractive to users.

- **Guidance**: Animations can effectively guide users through the intended flow of application use, highlighting interactive elements subtly.

- **Reward**: Interactive animations that respond to user actions can act as a reward mechanism, enhancing the satisfaction of interaction and encouraging further engagement.

Principles of Effective Animation Design

To optimize animations for feedback and engagement, they should be designed with specific principles in mind:

- **Appropriate Timing**: Ensure animations are neither too slow to cause delays nor too fast to be missed by users.

- **Understated Complexity**: Aim for simplicity to keep the user interface clean and focused, avoiding distractions.

- **Purpose-Driven**: Each animation should have a clear, definable purpose that contributes positively to the user experience.

Examples of Implementing UI Animations

To demonstrate how animations can be effectively used, let's explore practical examples in UI design:

Example 1: Button Interaction Animation

A common application is enhancing button interactions to provide visual feedback:

HTML:

```html
<button id="submitBtn">Submit</button>
```

CSS:

```css
#submitBtn {
    padding: 8px 15px;
    background-color: #4CAF50;
    color: white;
    border: none;
    border-radius: 3px;
    transition: background-color 0.3s ease;
}

#submitBtn:hover {
    background-color: #45a049;
}
```

This CSS subtly changes the button's background color on hover, signaling that it is clickable.

Example 2: Animated Loading Indicator

Visual indicators are crucial for operations that require a wait time, such as data loading:

HTML:

```html
<div id="loader"></div>
```

CSS:

```css
#loader {
  width: 40px;
  height: 40px;
  border: 4px solid #f3f3f3;
  border-top: 4px solid #3498db;
  border-radius: 50%;
  animation: spin 2s linear infinite;
}

@keyframes spin {
  0% { transform: rotate(0deg); }
  100% { transform: rotate(360deg); }
}
```

This setup provides a rotating loader animation, indicating that the application is processing the user's request.

Challenges in Animation Design

Designing animations that enhance both feedback and engagement involves challenges such as maintaining balance in animation timing and ensuring that the animations do not overpower the content or functionality.

Conclusion

Animations are a crucial feature in UI design, significantly affecting feedback mechanisms and user engagement. By carefully planning and implementing animations, designers can create more responsive, intuitive, and enjoyable digital environments. As technology progresses, the role of animation in user interfaces will likely become more innovative, further enhancing how users interact with digital products.

Chapter Seven

Enhancing User Engagement Through Storytelling

Narrative Techniques in UX Design

Narrative techniques in User Experience (UX) design play a critical role in deepening user engagement and enhancing the communicative effectiveness of digital products. By embedding storytelling elements into UX design, professionals can create a more cohesive and compelling user journey that not only facilitates information delivery but also enriches the overall user interaction. This article discusses the application of narrative strategies in UX design, detailing their advantages and demonstrating how they can be pragmatically incorporated to enrich user interfaces.

The Concept of Narrative in UX Design

Narrative UX involves applying storytelling principles to craft experiences that guide users through a product in a structured and engaging way. Key storytelling elements adapted for UX include:

1. **Character**: Often represented by the user, who is seen as the hero of the story.

2. **Setting**: The environment or platform where the user interacts with the product.

3. **Conflict**: Challenges or tasks that the user encounters while using the product.

4. **Resolution**: The solution or conclusion provided by the product that resolves the user's challenges.

Advantages of Using Narrative Techniques

Incorporating narrative elements into UX design can significantly enhance the interaction by:

- **Boosting User Engagement**: Narratives can capture the user's attention more effectively, making the experience memorable.

- **Improving Interface Usability**: Storytelling can make navigating through a product more intuitive.

- **Creating Emotional Connections**: Emotional engagement can be achieved by resonating with the user's feelings and experiences.

- **Enhancing User Satisfaction**: Users tend to appreciate products that not only meet their functional needs but also provide an enjoyable experience.

Strategies for Narrative Implementation

To effectively implement narrative techniques in UX design, consider the following strategies:

1. **Developing User Personas**: Crafting detailed personas can help in creating narratives that are deeply relatable and personalized.

2. **Mapping the Customer Journey**: This technique helps in visualizing the user's path and identifying opportunities for incorporating narrative elements.

3. **Employing Gamification**: Adding game mechanics like rewards and achievements can make the user journey feel more like a story with objectives and milestones.

4. **Strategic Content Development**: Writing content that follows a narrative structure can guide users fluidly through the functions of the product.

Example: Narrative-Driven Onboarding Experience

Consider an app designed to help users improve their productivity. The onboarding process can be framed as a quest where each task completed brings the user closer to mastering their time.

HTML Setup:

```html
<div id="welcomeMessage">
  <h1>Embark on Your Productivity Quest!</h1>
  <p>Unlock the secrets to becoming more efficient every day.</p>
  <button onclick="beginAdventure()">Begin Adventure</button>
</div>
```

CSS Styling:

```css
#welcomeMessage h1 {
  color: #34568B;
  text-align: center;
}
#welcomeMessage p {
  color: #6B7A8F;
  text-align: center;
}
button {
  background-color: #FF6F61;
  color: white;
  padding: 10px 20px;
  border-radius: 4px;
  cursor: pointer;
}
button:hover {
  background-color: #88B04B;
}
```

JavaScript for Interactive Elements:

```javascript
function beginAdventure() {
  // Code to initiate the onboarding sequence
  alert("Let the productivity journey begin!");
}
```

In this example, the welcoming narrative introduces the onboarding as a personal journey, making it immediately engaging and setting the stage for the user to explore the app's features.

Conclusion

Utilizing narrative techniques in UX design not only enhances the functionality of digital interfaces but also enriches the emotional and psychological user experience. By crafting compelling stories within the product design, UX designers can create more meaningful and engaging interactions that resonate well with users. As we continue to advance in digital design, narratives will increasingly serve as vital tools in creating distinctive and effective user experiences.

Creating Cohesive Brand Stories

In today's competitive marketplace, cohesive brand stories are crucial for establishing a brand's identity and enhancing connections with consumers. These stories integrate a company's values, mission, and visions into a narrative that resonates with audiences, fostering loyalty and setting the brand apart. This article examines the strategic implementation of narrative techniques in crafting brand stories, highlights their importance, and offers guidance on effective storytelling.

The Value of Cohesive Brand Stories

Brand stories that are well-articulated serve more than promotional purposes; they create emotional engagements, making the brand experience memorable and impactful.

Advantages of Well-Crafted Brand Stories:

- **Deeper User Engagement:** Narrative-driven content captures and retains consumer attention better than conventional marketing.

- **Better Brand Recall:** Memorable stories help brands stand out, enhancing recall in competitive environments.

- **Loyalty Building:** Stories that align with consumer values encourage deeper loyalty.

- **Competitive Differentiation:** Distinctive narratives differentiate a brand by clearly defining what it stands for.

Elements of Effective Brand Stories

Effective brand stories are composed of several elements that ensure the narrative is engaging and coherent:

1. **Core Message:** This encapsulates the primary message or value the brand wishes to communicate.

2. **Characterization:** Often, the brand itself is personified in the story, making it relatable to the audience.

3. **Conflict:** Essential to any story, this element involves the challenges or problems that the brand helps consumers overcome.

4. **Resolution:** How the brand effectively resolves conflicts, underscoring its importance and utility.

5. **Consistent Voice and Tone:** The narrative should maintain a consistent voice that reflects the brand's character across all media.

Strategies for Crafting Your Brand Story

Developing a cohesive brand story that effectively communicates your brand's essence involves several strategic steps:

1. **Clarify Core Values:** Define clear and strong values that are easy for audiences to understand and appreciate.

2. **Audience Insights:** A deep understanding of the target audience is critical. Tailor the narrative to meet their expectations and address their needs.

3. **Structured Narrative:** Create a compelling narrative with a clear beginning, development, and conclusion that guides consumers through the brand experience.

4. **Focus on Authenticity:** Ensure that the story is authentic and accurately represents the brand's true practices and goals.

Example: Implementing a Brand Story

Consider a fictional company specializing in eco-friendly packaging solutions.

Core Message: "Innovating packaging, preserving the planet."

Character and Conflict: The company, born from a commitment to environmental conservation, addresses the widespread problem of non-recyclable waste.

Resolution: By providing biodegradable packaging options, the company offers a practical solution to reducing environmental impact.

Narrative Deployment on a Website:

```html
<section id="ourMission">
  <h1>Our Green Mission</h1>
  <p>Join us on our journey to transform the packaging industry with solutions
     that care for the earth.</p>
</section>
```

CSS Styling:

```css
#ourMission {
  background-color: #e4f9f5;
  color: #205072;
  padding: 20px;
  font-family: 'Verdana', sans-serif;
}
```

This web section introduces the company's mission and vision, using narrative elements to engage visitors and encourage them to support the brand's environmental initiatives.

Conclusion

Creating a cohesive brand story is fundamental for meaningful consumer engagement and effective brand communication. By weaving values and missions into a compelling narrative, brands can enhance their market presence and foster enduring relationships with their audience. As storytelling continues to shape brand strategies, those who master this art will likely lead in their respective sectors.

Case Studies of Successful Story-driven Designs

Story-driven design has become a pivotal aspect of modern marketing and user experience strategies. It leverages narrative elements to create more engaging interactions and strengthen brand identity. This article explores several case studies where integrating storytelling into design practices has significantly improved customer engagement and shaped brand perceptions, providing valuable insights into the process and benefits of these approaches.

1. Airbnb: Embracing Local Experiences

Airbnb's 2016 "Live There" campaign successfully shifted its brand narrative from mere accommodation booking to enriching travel experiences. This approach aimed to distinguish Airbnb from traditional hotel services by promoting a deeper cultural immersion.

Strategy and Implementation: The campaign enhanced listings by incorporating hosts' stories and personal insights about their locales, effectively weaving these narratives into the user interface of both their website and app.

Outcome: The story-driven model fostered a stronger emotional connection between travelers and their destinations, significantly boosting engagement and increasing bookings. It positioned Airbnb not just as a service, but as a gateway to authentic local experiences.

2. Apple: Storytelling in Product Launches

Apple's approach to product launches is a masterclass in narrative integration. Each new device is introduced not just as a product but as a continuation of the Apple story, emphasizing innovation and lifestyle enhancement.

Strategy and Implementation: During their keynotes, Apple crafts a compelling narrative around each product, focusing on the journey of its creation, the challenges it addresses, and its impact on users' lives. This story is delivered through high-quality visuals and dynamic presentations that captivate the audience.

Outcome: This method has reinforced Apple's image as a pioneer in technology, making each product release highly anticipated events that effectively convert features into stories, thus driving consumer interest and loyalty.

3. Dove: The Real Beauty Campaign

Dove's "Real Beauty" campaign leveraged narrative techniques to challenge conventional beauty standards and promote inclusivity. Launched in 2004, it used real stories of diverse women to redefine beauty norms.

Strategy and Implementation: The campaign featured authentic stories and images of women of various ages and body types, shared across multiple media platforms. This not only created a unified narrative across all channels but also engaged consumers on a personal level.

Outcome: Dove not only saw a significant increase in product sales but also ignited a global discussion on beauty standards, enhancing its brand reputation as a socially conscious leader.

4. Google: The Impact of Google Doodles

Google Doodles are an excellent example of how daily micro-interactions can be transformed through storytelling. These unique reinterpretations of the Google logo celebrate notable historical figures and events, enhancing the user experience with fun, educational content.

Strategy and Implementation: A dedicated team designs these Doodles to be interactive, often incorporating games or animations that provide a brief diversion while educating users about significant occurrences or achievements.

Outcome: Google Doodles have successfully increased daily engagement with the search engine, making Google not just a utility but a part of users' daily discovery and learning processes.

Conclusion

These case studies demonstrate the transformative power of story-driven design across different industries. By embedding narratives into their branding and design strategies, companies can significantly enhance user engagement, set themselves apart in competitive markets, and create memorable brand experiences that resonate deeply with their audiences. As digital engagement continues to evolve, storytelling will remain a vital tool in crafting impactful and innovative user experiences.

Chapter Eight

Usability Testing at an Intermediate Level

Quantitative vs. Qualitative Methods

Differentiating between quantitative and qualitative research methodologies is vital for researchers aiming to align their study designs with specific investigative goals. These approaches serve distinct research purposes, offering unique benefits based on the nature of the inquiry. This article discusses the salient features of both quantitative and qualitative methods, exploring their ideal applications and distinguishing characteristics.

Describing Quantitative Methods

Quantitative research is hallmarked by its focus on structured data collection and its reliance on statistical tools for analysis. This method is employed primarily to quantify data, allowing for the establishment of patterns and numerical evidence to support hypotheses.

Key Characteristics:

- **Structured Measurement:** Quantitative research involves systematic, objective data collection methods, such as surveys with predefined answers and controlled experimental conditions.

- **Data Analysis:** It typically uses statistical tools to analyze numerical data, aiming to validate research hypotheses quantitatively.

- **Replicability:** The methodical nature of quantitative studies promotes consistency and reproducibility, crucial for verifying results.

Applications Include:

- Quantitative surveys that utilize Likert scales or similar metrics

- Experimental designs with variable manipulation

- Trend analysis over specified periods

Application Example: A tech company may deploy quantitative strategies to evaluate user engagement by statistically analyzing usage data collected through digital tracking tools.

Describing Qualitative Methods

Qualitative research seeks to provide depth and context to understand complex human behaviors and emotions. It employs more flexible, open-ended techniques to gather comprehensive and nuanced data.

Key Characteristics:

- **In-depth Exploration:** This approach focuses on collecting rich, descriptive data that delve deeply into participant experiences and motivations.

- **Subjective Analysis:** It values the insights gained from direct interactions, considering the unique perspectives of participants as essential to understanding the phenomena.

- **Natural Settings:** Qualitative research often occurs in real-world settings, enriching the data with contextual authenticity.

Applications Include:

- Detailed interviews that allow for expansive participant responses

- Observational studies within the participants' natural environment

- Discussion groups that explore diverse viewpoints on a topic

Application Example: Researchers might employ qualitative methods to study the impact of a community health initiative, conducting interviews and focus groups to gauge community members' perceptions and experiences.

Comparative Analysis

Choosing between quantitative and qualitative methods typically depends on the research objectives, the depth of analysis required, and the specificity of the data needed. Here's how they contrast:

- **Data Type:** Quantitative methods result in numeric data ideal for statistical testing, whereas qualitative methods produce rich, textual data suited for thematic analysis.

- **Collection Methodology:** Quantitative research employs static, structured data collection methods, while qualitative research uses dynamic, narrative-driven approaches.

- **Analytical Techniques:** Quantitative studies utilize statistical analyses; qualitative studies apply methods like narrative or content analysis.

- **Outcome Focus:** Quantitative research often seeks broad generalizability, whereas qualitative research provides detailed insights into specific contexts or groups.

Integrating Both Methods

Utilizing a combination of quantitative and qualitative methods can enrich a research study, providing both statistical breadth and in-depth narrative insight. This mixed-methods approach ensures a comprehensive exploration of the research topic.

Integration Example: In evaluating the effectiveness of new educational technology, quantitative methods could measure student performance improvements, while qualitative interviews with teachers could explore perceptions and experiences with the technology.

Conclusion

Quantitative and qualitative methodologies each have distinct advantages and are chosen based on the specific requirements of the research project. By selecting the appropriate approach, or a combination thereof, researchers can ensure that their studies are robust and insightful. These methodologies are indispensable tools for advancing knowledge in a wide range of academic and practical fields.

Advanced Testing Tools and Techniques

In the rapidly evolving software development sector, the use of advanced testing tools and techniques is crucial for validating software functionality and adherence to quality standards. These sophisticated tools streamline the testing process and significantly enhance the accuracy of results, ensuring software performance across different scenarios. This article will review a variety of top-tier testing tools and methodologies, exploring their roles, advantages, and how they fit into the software development cycle.

1. Automated Testing Tools

Automated testing tools are pivotal in modern testing strategies, automating the execution of test cases to increase efficiency and reduce reliance on manual testing. These tools replicate user interactions and rigorously assess application functionalities across multiple scenarios.

Principal Automated Testing Tools:

- **Selenium:** An open-source automation framework that supports a wide range of browsers and operating systems, ideal for web application testing.

- **Appium:** A mobile testing tool that facilitates automation for both Android and iOS applications.

- **TestComplete:** This tool allows for easy automation of tests across web, mobile, and desktop platforms, suitable for users with varying levels of technical expertise.

Example of Using Selenium:

```python
from selenium import webdriver

driver = webdriver.Chrome()
driver.get("http://www.example.com")
login_button = driver.find_element_by_id('login')
login_button.click()
assert "Dashboard" in driver.title
driver.quit()
```

This script showcases how Selenium can automate typical browser tasks such as navigating a website, clicking elements, and verifying page titles, simplifying the testing process.

2. CI/CD Tools

CI/CD tools are critical components in contemporary software development, automating testing and deployment processes. These tools enable immediate testing and feedback on code changes, enhancing the quality and efficiency of software development.

Key CI/CD Tools:

- **Jenkins:** A powerful open-source automation server that enhances continuous integration and continuous delivery processes.

- **CircleCI:** Noted for its rapid setup and execution, it is particularly well-suited for agile development environments.

- **GitLab CI:** Integrated within the GitLab platform, it offers streamlined CI/CD capabilities that enhance productivity and workflow.

3. Performance Testing Tools

These tools are essential for assessing how applications perform under stress, evaluating their responsiveness, scalability, and stability under various load conditions.

Leading Performance Testing Tools:

- **LoadRunner:** Used extensively for simulating user interactions to test the application's load handling capabilities.

- **JMeter:** Popular for its robust performance testing and load simulation capabilities across different service types.

- **Gatling:** Renowned for its efficiency in load and stress testing, especially for web applications.

4. Security Testing Tools

Security testing tools are indispensable for identifying potential security vulnerabilities that could compromise application integrity and user data.

Essential Security Testing Tools:

- **OWASP ZAP:** Targets vulnerabilities in web applications to enhance security.

- **Burp Suite:** Offers a suite of web application security testing tools, widely used for its depth of features.

- **Fortify:** Known for its comprehensive security scans, it helps in detecting and mitigating security vulnerabilities accurately.

5. Code Quality and Review Tools

These tools analyze source code to identify bugs, vulnerabilities, and other issues that may affect software performance and maintainability.

Prominent Tools for Code Quality:

- **SonarQube:** Provides detailed insights into code quality, offering metrics and analytics.

- **Coverity:** Known for its effective static code analysis, which helps in identifying code defects.

- **CodeClimate:** Reviews code to identify potential maintainability issues, providing insights into code complexity and test coverage.

Advantages of Advanced Testing Techniques

- **Increased Precision:** Automation minimizes manual errors, enhancing test precision.

- **Enhanced Efficiency:** Automation and CI/CD tools quicken the testing process, optimizing resource use.

- **Comprehensive Testing:** Advanced tools enable simulation of various user scenarios, ensuring thorough testing coverage.

- **Early Issue Identification:** Integrating testing early in the development process helps detect issues promptly, reducing remediation costs.

Conclusion

The integration of advanced testing tools and techniques is essential for modern software development practices, ensuring that products meet expected quality benchmarks and function reliably under diverse conditions. Continuously updating with the latest advancements in testing technologies is crucial for developers to deliver high-quality, secure, and efficient software while maintaining competitiveness in the technology industry.

Interpreting Data to Refine Interfaces

In the fast-paced world of digital development, employing data-driven approaches in interface design is crucial for maximizing user engagement and operational effectiveness. These strategies rely on precise data from user interactions to inform and validate design decisions, significantly enhancing interface functionality. This discussion will explore the role of data interpretation in refining interfaces, identify the key types of data involved, and describe the processes used to leverage these insights for design optimization.

The Critical Role of Data in Interface Design

Interfaces serve as the primary means for user interaction with digital platforms, making their design critical for user experience. Using data-driven methods ensures that design adjustments are rooted in actual user behavior, thereby optimizing both visual and functional aspects of interfaces. Systematic analysis of interaction data enables designers to spot and rectify usability issues, tailor interfaces to better meet user needs, and ultimately, improve overall user satisfaction.

Data Utilized in Interface Optimization

1. **Behavioral Metrics**: Data such as user click-through rates, path tracking, session duration, and feature utilization are vital. Analytical tools, notably Google Analytics, provide these metrics, offering a solid basis for understanding user engagement.

2. **Visual Interaction Maps**: Tools like Hotjar and Crazy Egg utilize heatmaps to illustrate user interaction across a page, identifying zones of high activity and sections that fail to capture attention.

3. **Qualitative User Feedback**: Insights from user surveys, feedback forms, and structured interviews deliver crucial qualitative data that highlights user needs and areas for improvement.

4. **Experimental Data from A/B Testing**: This involves presenting variants of a page or feature to users to scientifically determine which variations yield better usability and user satisfaction.

Methodology for Data-Driven Interface Refinement

Enhancing interfaces based on data involves a detailed and iterative process:

1. **Data Collection**: Initial deployment of tools and methods for capturing relevant user interaction data.

2. **Thorough Data Analysis**: Teams analyze this data to detect patterns, anomalies, and user experience issues that could benefit from design adjustments.

3. **Hypothesis Formulation**: Based on the insights gained, hypotheses regarding potential enhancements are crafted, proposing specific changes aimed at improving user interaction.

4. **Design Implementation and Testing**: Proposed changes are implemented in the interface, and A/B testing is conducted to assess the effectiveness of these modifications in real-world scenarios.

5. **Evaluation and Iteration**: Following testing, results are evaluated to determine whether the changes positively impacted user experience, with subsequent adjustments made based on this feedback.

Example Scenario: Streamlining a Media Streaming Service Interface

Consider a scenario where a media streaming service experiences low engagement on its viewer interface. The approach to enhancing this could involve:

- **Step 1: Data Collection**

  o Implementing tools to track viewer interactions and engagement levels on the interface.

  o Setting up heatmaps to observe user activity patterns.

- **Step 2: Analyzing the Data**

  o Analysis reveals underutilization of search functionalities and navigation issues.

- **Step 3: Hypothesis Development**

  o It's hypothesized that enhancing the visibility and functionality of the search feature could improve engagement.

- **Step 4: Implementation and Testing**

  o Redesigning the search interface for greater prominence and ease of use.

  o Running A/B tests to compare user engagement with the new versus the old design.

- **Step 5: Review and Final Adjustments**

  o If the new design demonstrates a marked improvement in engagement metrics, it is adopted. Otherwise, further tweaks are tested.

Conclusion

Utilizing data to refine interfaces is an essential strategy in modern digital design, significantly affecting user satisfaction and interface efficiency. As interface design continues to evolve, the importance of a data-driven approach becomes increasingly significant, highlighting the need for ongoing adaptation and innovation in design practices. This methodology not only ensures interfaces are appealing but also guarantees they are optimally functional and user-centric.

Chapter Nine

Advanced Prototyping Tools and Techniques

Using Higher-Fidelity Prototypes

In product design and software development, the utility of higher-fidelity prototypes cannot be overstated. These advanced prototypes, which closely simulate the final product in both appearance and functionality, are indispensable in refining design processes. They allow for a detailed exploration of how products will interact with end-users by integrating complex user interfaces, interactions, and realistic content. This article examines the advantages of utilizing higher-fidelity prototypes, their role in enhancing user testing, and strategies for effective implementation within development workflows.

Overview of Higher-Fidelity Prototypes

Higher-fidelity prototypes are sophisticated models that provide a near-complete representation of the final product, offering interactive elements and detailed aesthetics. These prototypes differ significantly from low-fidelity prototypes, such as paper models or basic wireframes, by providing a comprehensive, interactive experience that includes detailed UI elements, intricate animations, and even backend integration.

Creation of such prototypes often involves tools designed for intricate design and interaction:

- **Axure RP**: Facilitates complex interactive prototypes with logical conditions and dynamic content.

- **Adobe XD**: Supports detailed vector-based designs and allows for prototyping with advanced transitions and collaborative feedback.

- **Figma**: Popular for its powerful interactive design capabilities and collaborative functions, making it a top choice among UX/UI professionals.

Advantages of High-Fidelity Prototyping

1. **Rich User Feedback**: High-fidelity prototypes offer a realistic user experience that elicits specific, actionable feedback during testing phases. Users engage with the prototype in a manner akin to the final product, yielding insights that are directly applicable to design improvements.

2. **Clear Stakeholder Communication**: These prototypes are particularly effective in demonstrating design intentions and functionality to stakeholders. By presenting tangible, interactive designs, they help in aligning expectations and securing stakeholder approval.

3. **Identification of Usability Flaws**: Including real-world workflows and interactions in these prototypes allows design teams to detect and address user experience issues early, thereby reducing later development costs.

4. **Assessment of Technical Feasibility**: Higher-fidelity prototypes can be integrated with actual backend services to evaluate the design's technical viability, including load performance, data handling, and system interactions.

Deploying High-Fidelity Prototypes in Development

Integrating high-fidelity prototypes into development involves several critical steps:

1. **Base Design and Wireframing**: Begin with fundamental layouts that define the structure and core components of the application.

2. **Increasing Fidelity**: Progressively incorporate visual enhancements and interactive elements using tools like Figma or Adobe XD, which facilitate detailed design and user interaction simulations.

3. **Technical Integration and Testing**: For prototypes meant to simulate web interactions, connecting the frontend design to APIs or mock backends is crucial. For example:

```
// Simulating API integration in a prototype
fetch('https://api.example.com/data')
  .then(response => response.json())
  .then(data => console.log(data))
  .catch(error => console.error('Error:', error));
```

This code snippet demonstrates how to incorporate API calls into a prototype, enabling realistic data interactions and testing user scenarios within the design.

4. **User Testing and Refinement**: Conduct user testing sessions to observe interactions and gather feedback, iterating on the design based on these insights before moving to final development.

Challenges and Considerations

While high-fidelity prototypes are highly beneficial, they require significant resources and time to develop. Design teams must manage the detailed creation process without excessively prolonging the development timeline. Additionally, there is a risk that stakeholders may become too attached to specific features of the prototype, which could restrict flexibility in responding to user feedback.

Conclusion

High-fidelity prototypes are vital assets in the design toolkit, providing critical insights that enhance user interfaces and overall product functionality. Although resource-intensive, the depth of feedback and testing accuracy they offer can significantly smooth the development process, leading to products that are both effective and user-centric. Properly integrated into the design and development phases, high-fidelity prototypes can substantially elevate the quality and success of the final product.

Simulating User Interactions and Transitions

In contemporary interface design, simulating user interactions and transitions is essential for crafting interfaces that are intuitive and appealing. These simulations enhance the usability of the user experience during development phases and provide critical insights into how end-users will interact with the final product. This article explores the importance of such simulations, outlines effective methodologies, and presents coding examples to illustrate integration into software development.

The Role of Simulating User Interactions and Transitions

Simulating user interactions and transitions is crucial for several fundamental aspects:

- **Usability Analysis**: It enables designers to test the interface's user-friendliness and intuitive design before completion.

- **Feedback Collection**: By showcasing a working model of the product to stakeholders and test users, simulations gather detailed feedback to refine the interface.

- **Problem Detection**: Early simulation can uncover potential issues with design or functionality, reducing later costs by addressing these issues early in the development process.

Tools and Techniques for Effective Simulations

Several tools and methodologies facilitate the simulation of user interactions and transitions:

- **Prototyping Tools**: Applications like Axure RP, Figma, and Adobe XD are equipped to create dynamic, high-fidelity prototypes that simulate the final product's interactive experience.

- **Interactive Development Environments**: Frameworks such as ReactJS and AngularJS are used to develop responsive interfaces that mimic true user interaction.

Implementing Interaction Simulations

1. **Storyboarding**: This preliminary phase involves visually plotting user interactions to guide the design process.

2. **Interactive Prototyping**: Using advanced tools like Adobe XD, designers build interactive prototypes that closely mimic the final interface, allowing for user testing and interaction.

3. **Animation Integration**: Adding detailed animations through libraries like GreenSock Animation Platform (GSAP) or Animate.css enhances the realism of transitions and user interactions within prototypes.

Example Code Snippets

Simulations often require scripts that respond to user actions such as mouse clicks or screen touches. Below are examples that utilize JavaScript and GSAP to simulate user interactions and transitions:

JavaScript for User Interactions:

```
document.getElementById("confirmButton").addEventListener("click", function() {
    document.getElementById("successMessage").style.display = "block";
    alert("Your action has been confirmed!");
});
```

This code sets up an event listener on a confirmation button that triggers a display change and an alert when clicked, mimicking a real user action.

GSAP for Animated Transitions:

```
gsap.to("#modalWindow", {duration: 1.5, scaleX: 1, scaleY: 1, ease: "power2.inOut"});
```

Here, GSAP is used to animate a modal window, scaling it smoothly to draw user attention, simulating a transition effect found in high-end interfaces.

Best Practices for Simulation

- **Consistency Is Key**: Keeping interaction and transition styles consistent throughout the application enhances user understanding and comfort.

- **Optimize Performance**: Ensure simulations are optimized for performance to avoid lag, which can negatively impact the user experience.

- **Realistic Design Choices**: Simulations should be based on actual user data and behavior to ensure they are realistic and relevant.

- **Iterative Approach**: Continuously refine simulations based on user feedback, improving the interface incrementally to better meet user needs.

Conclusion

Simulating user interactions and transitions is a critical element in developing effective user interfaces. Through the use of sophisticated prototyping tools and strategic implementation of feedback, developers and designers can ensure that interfaces are not only aesthetically pleasing but also highly functional. This process is key to developing products that successfully meet user expectations and perform reliably in real-world scenarios, ultimately leading to enhanced user satisfaction and engagement.

Integrative Tools for Rapid Prototyping

Rapid prototyping plays a pivotal role in the modern landscape of software engineering and product design, expediting design iterations and enhancing product iterations through quick feedback and validation. Integrative tools specialized for rapid prototyping streamline this entire process, allowing for swift visualization, testing, and tweaking of ideas. This article outlines the utility of such tools, their benefits, key functionalities, and their implementation within the development process.

Utility of Integrative Tools in Rapid Prototyping

Integrative prototyping tools are engineered to link various phases of product development, from initial concept to final implementation, ensuring smooth transitions across different stages. These tools are designed to be inherently collaborative, accommodating the diverse roles within a team—designers, developers, and stakeholders—to collectively refine and evolve the product.

Benefits of Employing Integrative Prototyping Tools

1. **Speed**: These tools significantly decrease the duration from concept to prototype, enabling faster iteration and feedback cycles.

2. **Collaboration Enhancement**: They offer collaborative functionalities that enable real-time teamwork across different departments and geographical locations.

3. **Uniform Design**: Through the use of reusable assets and consistent design systems, these tools help maintain uniformity across multiple projects.

4. **Agility**: Flexible design modifications are possible, allowing teams to quickly adapt based on ongoing feedback, maintaining agility in the development process.

Prominent Tools for Integrative Rapid Prototyping

The market offers several standout tools known for their extensive features and ability to integrate across different platforms:

- **Figma**: Renowned for its user-friendly interface that allows simultaneous collaboration, Figma integrates seamlessly with other tools, enhancing its utility in prototyping and feedback integration.

- **InVision**: With a comprehensive suite of design and prototyping functionalities, InVision is compatible with other major design programs like Sketch and Adobe

XD, making it ideal for detailed prototypes requiring animated interactions.

- **Adobe XD**: This tool merges various design functions such as wireframing, visual design, and prototyping into one streamlined application. It supports complex interactive elements vital for contemporary interface design.

- **Axure RP**: Preferred for its capability to simulate detailed interactive prototypes that involve conditional logic and calculations, Axure RP is invaluable for creating sophisticated prototypes without the need for coding.

Implementation Examples and Techniques

Integrating these tools typically follows a structured process from initial design to user testing and final refinement. Below is an example of how interactive elements might be implemented in Adobe XD:

Example: Configuring an Interactive Button in Adobe XD

1. **Design Setup**: Use the shape tool to create a button, customize its properties like size and color, and label it using the text tool.

2. **Prototyping Interaction**: Link the button to another artboard within the prototype to simulate navigation through interaction settings.

3. **Interaction Specification**: Specify the type of interaction (e.g., Tap) and select an appropriate

animation effect (e.g., dissolve) for transitioning to the next page.

4. **Testing and Review**: Utilize Adobe XD's preview functionality to test the interaction and share the prototype for feedback.

```javascript
// Example code for a clickable button in a web-based prototype
document.querySelector('#myButton').addEventListener('click', function() {
    document.querySelector('#nextPage').style.display = 'block'; // Activate the
        next page display
});
```

This JavaScript snippet demonstrates how to implement a clickable button that leads to another page, simulating a typical navigation interaction in a web environment.

Conclusion

Integrative tools for rapid prototyping are reshaping how digital products are designed and developed, allowing teams to work more efficiently and responsively. By utilizing tools such as Figma, InVision, Adobe XD, and Axure RP, teams can rapidly prototype, gather feedback, and refine products, ensuring they meet market demands and user expectations effectively. As these tools continue to evolve, they will further enhance the capabilities of teams to innovate and refine their products efficiently.

Chapter Ten

Design Systems and Style Guides

Developing and Maintaining Design Systems

Design systems are integral in today's realm of product development, providing crucial frameworks that ensure consistency, efficiency, and scalability. These systems compile components, patterns, and guidelines that simplify the design process and encourage collaboration among teams. This article outlines the approaches and practices for crafting and sustaining effective design systems.

Significance of Design Systems

Design systems act as comprehensive references for design and development teams, fostering uniformity and cohesion across products. Key benefits include:

1. **Consistency**: They standardize design elements across projects and platforms, enhancing user experiences.

2. **Efficiency**: Design systems allow for the reuse of components, streamlining both design and development workflows.

3. **Scalability**: Centralized design guidelines and components facilitate straightforward updates and expansion.

Essential Elements of a Design System

A robust design system generally encompasses:

1. **Design Principles**: Foundational guidelines that articulate the design ethos, aligning all design efforts with the brand's objectives and user needs.

2. **UI Components**: Standardized reusable elements like buttons, input fields, and navigational structures ensure visual and functional consistency.

3. **Patterns**: Documented solutions to frequent design challenges (e.g., grid systems, typographic scales, responsive strategies).

4. **Style Guide**: A manual detailing the visual language, including color palettes, typography, and spacing specifications.

5. **Code Libraries**: Repositories of pre-written front-end code that correspond to the visual components, facilitating swift development implementation.

Steps to Develop a Design System

1. **Evaluation and Strategy**: Initiate by reviewing current design practices and assets to pinpoint discrepancies and redundancies. Outline the design system's scope, objectives, and foundational principles.

2. **Component Development**: Construct a suite of flexible, reusable UI components. Each component, like a button, should accommodate different states and styles to maximize usability and adaptability.

```
// Example React component for a button
const Button = ({ type = 'primary', disabled = false, onClick, children }) => {
    const className = `btn ${type} ${disabled ? 'disabled' : ''}`;
    return (
        <button className={className} onClick={onClick} disabled={disabled}>
            {children}
        </button>
    );
};
```

3. **Style Guide Creation**: Compile a comprehensive style guide that includes detailed design specifications to guide consistent application.

4. **Pattern Documentation**: Identify and document reusable design patterns that address common issues, providing clear examples for application.

5. **System Documentation and Management**: Utilize tools like Storybook, Figma, or Sketch for documenting and managing the design system. Ensure the documentation is comprehensive and accessible.

```
// Markdown documentation for a button component
# Button Component
Utilized for user actions, available in several styles:
  **Primary**: Main action button.
  **Secondary**: Secondary action.
  **Disabled**: Indicates unavailability.

```jsx
<Button type="primary">Primary Button</Button>
<Button type="secondary">Secondary Button</Button>
<Button disabled>Disabled Button</Button>
```
```

Sustaining a Design System

1. **Continuous Updates**: Regularly update the system to reflect brand evolution or design trends. Implement systematic audits and maintain open feedback channels.

2. **Version Management**: Use version control systems like Git to document revisions and maintain historical integrity.

3. **Education and Integration**: Conduct training sessions and promote the system's integration into daily operations to ensure widespread adoption.

4. **Feedback Incorporation**: Establish feedback mechanisms to gather insights from users and stakeholders, essential for iterative improvement.

5. **Governance**: Implement a governance structure detailing the roles and responsibilities associated with the system's upkeep to ensure accountability.

Conclusion

Developing and maintaining a design system requires ongoing commitment to collaboration, updates, and adherence to established guidelines. By instituting a comprehensive design system, organizations can improve their product development cycles, ensuring a unified user experience across their product lineup. This structured approach not only elevates the quality and consistency of outputs but also enhances team efficiency and collaboration.

Consistency Across Multi-platform Interfaces

In the evolving landscape of technology, maintaining consistency across multi-platform interfaces is vital for delivering a uniform user experience. As organizations expand their digital footprint across various devices such as desktops, smartphones, and tablets, consistent interface design is crucial. This article discusses the benefits of consistent interfaces, strategies for achieving uniformity, and technical approaches to facilitate these strategies.

Benefits of Consistency in Multi-platform Interfaces

Uniform interfaces across different platforms yield several advantages:

1. **Enhanced User Experience**: Consistency allows users to seamlessly navigate between devices, improving usability and familiarity.

2. **Reinforced Brand Identity**: Maintaining consistent design elements like logos, color schemes, and layouts across platforms enhances brand recognition.

3. **Optimized Development Process**: Using shared design components and code across platforms accelerates development timelines and reduces costs.

Strategies for Achieving Consistency

Achieving consistency across interfaces requires strategic planning and execution:

1. **Comprehensive Design Language**: Create a design language that spans all platforms, incorporating

consistent styles, components, and interaction patterns while maintaining fundamental design principles.

2. **Use of Responsive and Adaptive Design**: Implement responsive design to ensure applications are effective across different screen sizes. Supplement this with adaptive design strategies that cater to specific platform features.

3. **Component-Based Approach**: Embrace a component-based development approach, where UI elements are designed as reusable modules. This ensures design continuity and expedites development.

4. **Employment of Cross-Platform Frameworks**: Utilize frameworks such as React Native or Flutter to support a single codebase for multiple platforms, simplifying maintenance and enhancing consistency.

5. **Systematic Testing Across Platforms**: Regularly test the interface on all platforms to ensure they function and appear consistently. Synchronize updates across platforms to preserve uniformity.

Technical Methods for Enforcing Consistency

Several practical techniques are essential for maintaining design consistency across platforms:

1. **Consistent Styling for Web and Mobile**: Employ CSS for web interfaces to ensure uniform styling. For mobile platforms, frameworks that support CSS-like styling can be applied to maintain consistency across iOS and Android.

```css
/* CSS example for consistent web styling */
.button {
    background-color: #007BFF;
    color: white;
    padding: 15px 25px;
    border: none;
    border-radius: 5px;
    text-align: center;
}
```

```javascript
// React Native styling for mobile interfaces
const styles = StyleSheet.create({
    button: {
        backgroundColor: '#007BFF',
        color: 'white',
        padding: 15,
        borderRadius: 5,
    },
});
```

2. **Design Tokens**: Use design tokens to manage and standardize design properties like colors and fonts across different technologies.

```json
// Design tokens example
{
    "color": {
        "brand": "#007BFF",
        "accent": "#FFFFFF"
    },
    "font": {
        "base": "16px",
        "large": "24px"
    }
}
```

3. **Component Libraries**: Integrate or develop component libraries that ensure consistency across platforms. Tools like Storybook can assist in building

119

and testing UI components that are consistent regardless of the platform.

4. **Automated Cross-Platform Testing**: Leverage tools such as Selenium for web and Appium for mobile to automate testing, ensuring that interfaces behave consistently across platforms.

Challenges in Consistency

Maintaining uniformity across platforms can be challenging due to:

- **Platform-Specific Design Guidelines**: Each platform often has its own design standards, which can conflict with efforts to maintain a uniform design.

- **Varied Device Performances**: Different device capabilities can affect application performance, complicating consistent delivery.

- **Resource Distribution**: Efficiently allocating resources to support design consistency across platforms can be challenging, especially in resource-limited situations.

Conclusion

Ensuring consistency across multi-platform interfaces is essential for a seamless user experience, strengthening brand identity, and streamlining development practices. By developing a unified design language, employing cross-platform frameworks, and adopting a component-based architecture, organizations can achieve effective and consistent user interfaces across all digital touchpoints.

Regular testing and the strategic use of design tokens play crucial roles in navigating the complexities associated with diverse platforms and device types.

Style Guides as a UX Tool

In the field of user experience (UX) design, style guides are indispensable tools that set forth comprehensive guidelines for achieving visual and functional consistency across digital products. These guides are essential for design and development teams to uniformly apply a brand's design ethos. This article outlines the significance of style guides in UX design, elaborates on their key components, and explains how they contribute to a cohesive user experience.

Role of Style Guides in UX Design

Style guides are foundational in UX design for establishing clear standards regarding how products should look and operate. The primary advantages of employing a robust style guide include:

1. **Consistency**: Style guides ensure that all elements of a product consistently align, delivering a cohesive experience that aids user familiarity and comfort.

2. **Efficiency**: They expedite the design process by providing a clear set of rules for designers and developers, thereby minimizing the time and resources dedicated to decision-making.

3. **Scalability**: As products evolve and teams grow, style guides facilitate consistency management without

constant oversight, easing the integration of new features and team members.

4. **Brand Identity**: They reinforce brand identity by ensuring that every component of the product reflects the brand's visual and interaction principles.

Elements of a Style Guide

A thorough style guide for UX encompasses several elements that dictate the visual and functional aspects of a product's design:

1. **Visual Design Elements**

   o **Color Palette**: Specifies the primary and secondary color schemes that should visually represent the brand.

   o **Typography**: Details the typefaces, sizes, and letter spacing that ensure legibility and aesthetic harmony.

   o **Imagery and Icons**: Sets standards for the style, usage, and adaptation of images and icons to fit the brand's identity.

2. **UI Components**

   o **Buttons and Inputs**: Describes the appearance and behavior of interactive elements like buttons and input fields, including their different states.

   o **Navigation**: Provides specifications for designing navigation systems that are both intuitive and accessible.

3. **Interaction Design**

   o **Motion and Animation**: Establishes guidelines for animations and transitions that subtly enhance interactions without causing distractions.

   o **Feedback**: Outlines how the system should visually or audibly respond to user actions to provide clear and immediate feedback.

4. **Accessibility Standards**

   o **Contrast and Size**: Ensures all text and interactive elements comply with accessibility standards for visibility and usability.

   o **Keyboard Navigation**: Details specifications for products to support keyboard-only navigation, accommodating users with diverse abilities.

Implementing Style Guides in UX Projects

Effective implementation of a style guide in UX projects involves several practical steps:

1. **Development and Documentation**: Initiate the style guide creation with a collaborative effort among designers, developers, and product managers to cover all essential aspects. Ensure thorough documentation and accessibility for all team members.

Example CSS for a standardized button style:

```css
.button {
    background-color: var(--primary-color);
    color: white;
    padding: 10px 20px;
    border: none;
    border-radius: 3px;
    font-family: 'Arial', sans-serif;
    text-transform: uppercase;
    transition: background-color 0.2s;
}

.button:hover {
    background-color: var(--secondary-color);
}
```

2. **Regular Updates and Governance**: View the style guide as a living document that needs periodic updates to remain relevant as the brand and technology evolve. Set up a governance model to manage these updates.

3. **Tool Integration**: Seamlessly integrate the style guide into the tools and platforms utilized by the teams, such as design software tools like Figma or Adobe XD, to streamline the design process.

4. **Training and Advocacy**: Ensure widespread understanding and use of the style guide through regular educational workshops and advocacy to emphasize its importance.

Conclusion

Style guides are vital UX tools that ensure digital products are not only visually appealing but also functionally consistent and true to the brand identity. By establishing detailed guidelines on design and interaction, style guides streamline the user experience and the design process. Keeping a style guide current requires continuous updates and strong governance but is crucial for the success of UX projects, ensuring that user interfaces are effective and engaging.

Chapter Eleven

UX Writing and Content Strategy

The Role of Content in UX

In the digital design ecosystem, user experience (UX) transcends graphical elements, significantly involving content. This content ranges from texts and images to videos and other interactive media, serving to communicate a brand's ethos and facilitate user interactions within applications. This article examines the indispensable role content plays in UX, illustrating how it influences user interactions, shapes perceptions, and boosts both the functionality and accessibility of digital platforms.

Overview of Content in UX

In UX, content encompasses all informational elements displayed on a digital platform, from detailed texts like blog entries and product specifics to multimedia elements such as graphics and video content. This content is critical not just for relaying information but also for assisting users in navigating through an interface and effectively interacting with digital products.

Content as a Communicative Tool

The foremost role of content in UX is to facilitate clear and effective communication with users. Content is pivotal for explaining the purpose of digital products and guiding users on their usage. Properly organized content not only enhances user understanding but also optimizes interactions. Consider an example of how HTML content can be structured to enhance accessibility and clarity:

```html
<article>
    <h1>Explore Our Features</h1>
    <p>Unlock the full potential of your projects with our comprehensive suite of
        tools. Below are some key features:</p>
    <section>
        <h2>Robust Project Management</h2>
        <p>Streamline your projects with our state-of-the-art management tools
            .</p>
    </section>
    <section>
        <h2>Dynamic Collaboration</h2>
        <p>Collaborate with your team dynamically, across any distance.</p>
    </section>
</article>
```

This code example not only presents the content in a logical order but also employs semantic HTML elements to improve search engine optimization and accessibility.

Enhancing User Engagement

Content significantly enhances user engagement by making interactions with the product more interesting and interactive. Techniques such as storytelling or the inclusion of interactive narratives can deepen user engagement, making their experience with the product more profound and memorable.

Directing User Behavior

Content strategically guides user behavior, nudging them towards desired actions. Effective calls to action (CTAs), crucial elements of content strategy, are crafted to provoke specific user responses. Their success hinges on the clarity and appeal of their content:

```
<!-- Example of a call to action designed for maximum impact -->
<button onclick="startYourTrial()">Start Your Free Trial</button>
<script>
function startYourTrial() {
    // Logic to handle trial activation
}
</script>
```

This CTA is strategically placed to follow content that highlights the benefits of starting a trial, thus enhancing the likelihood of engagement.

Facilitating Usability and Accessibility

Content also significantly contributes to the usability and accessibility of digital products. Precise and clear content in the form of labels, descriptions, and navigational aids enhances interface navigability, especially for users with disabilities:

```
<!-- Example of content aimed at improving accessibility -->
<img src="example.jpg" alt="Elaborate description for visual content">
```

This inclusion of descriptive alt text ensures that visual content is accessible to users reliant on screen readers, thus improving overall accessibility.

Conclusion

Content's role in UX is multifaceted, impacting not just how information is delivered but also enhancing user interaction with digital products. Effective content strategy is crucial for delivering a seamless and inclusive user experience. By designing content meticulously, digital product designers ensure not only effective communication but also a positive, impactful user journey, reaffirming the vital role of content in UX design.

Techniques for Effective UX Writing

UX writing is crucial in user experience design, aimed at creating text that facilitates user interactions with digital interfaces. Effective UX writing clarifies navigation and functions, greatly improving user satisfaction by making digital products more intuitive. This article outlines various techniques for proficient UX writing, emphasizing how these strategies enhance user engagement and product usability.

The Essence of UX Writing

UX writing involves all text visible within software applications, websites, and other digital interfaces, from button labels to error messages and guide texts. It distinguishes itself from traditional copywriting by focusing primarily on user guidance and interface usability, rather than promotion or sales.

Strategies for Proficient UX Writing

1. **Clarity and Brevity** UX writing should be clear and concise to avoid user confusion and fatigue. Messages need to be straightforward, eliminating any unnecessary words. For instance:

```
<!-- Before: Wordy and unclear -->
<button>Advance to finalize your order</button>

<!-- After: Clear and concise -->
<button>Checkout</button>
```

The revised button text simplifies the action, making it quicker and easier for users to proceed.

2. **Consistency** Consistency in UX writing reinforces user learning and comfort. Using the same terms and phrases throughout an interface helps prevent confusion. For example, stick to either "cart" or "basket" throughout a website to maintain this consistency.

3. **User-Centric Language** UX writing should directly engage with the user by employing an active voice and directly addressing the user, making instructions clear and engaging:

```
<!-- Passive and impersonal -->
<p>The document was saved successfully.</p>

<!-- Active and personal -->
<p>You've successfully saved the document.</p>
```

The active voice in the second example makes the interaction more direct and personal.

4. **Effective Error Messages** Error messages in UX writing should do more than just alert the user to an issue; they should offer solutions or next steps. Clear and constructive error communication can enhance user experience by easing problem resolution:

```
<!-- Unhelpful error message -->
<p>Error: 404</p>

<!-- Helpful error message -->
<p>Oops! We can't find that page. Check the URL or head back to our <a href="/"
    >homepage</a>.</p>
```

This message not only explains the error but also guides the user on how to proceed.

5. **Accessibility in Writing** UX writing must be accessible to all users, including those with disabilities. Simple, clear language, free of jargon, ensures the content is comprehensible by everyone. Accommodations for screen readers and other assistive technologies should be made:

```
<!-- Example of accessible image text -->
<img src="welcome.jpg" alt="Welcome banner with cheerful greeter">
```

Including descriptive alt text for images enhances content accessibility.

6. **Design for Scannability** Most users scan text rather than reading it thoroughly. UX writing should be organized for easy scanning through the use of headings, bullet points, and concise paragraphs:

```
<h1>Key Benefits</h1>
<ul>
    <li>Simple setup process</li>
    <li>Intuitive design</li>
    <li>24/7 customer support</li>
</ul>
```

This structure allows users to quickly grasp essential information, improving content utility.

Conclusion

Effective UX writing is essential for creating enjoyable and efficient digital experiences. By employing techniques like clarity, consistency, direct user engagement, helpful error messaging, accessibility, and scannable layout, UX writers can significantly enhance the functionality and appeal of digital interfaces. These practices ensure that digital products are not only user-friendly but also engaging, encouraging better user interactions and satisfaction.

Aligning Content Strategy with User Expectations

Aligning content strategy with user expectations is critical for ensuring that digital platforms like websites and apps not only attract but also retain users. This alignment fosters enhanced user engagement, increases satisfaction, and strengthens brand loyalty by meeting users' informational and usability needs. This article explores the importance of syncing content strategy with user expectations and offers effective strategies to achieve this harmony.

Decoding User Expectations

User expectations encompass the preconceived notions and requirements users have when interacting with digital interfaces. These expectations are shaped by their past experiences, the brand's messaging, and overall market reputation. Understanding these can be pivotal in developing content that effectively resonates with and meets user needs.

Empirical Research and Analytics: Employing techniques such as user surveys, analytics, and usability tests can provide deep insights into user expectations. For instance, analytics platforms like Google Analytics help identify which content users find most engaging and why.

Strategies to Sync Content with User Expectations

1. **Creating User Personas**: Building detailed user personas based on genuine data is vital. These personas should reflect various user demographics, goals, frustrations, and preferred content, tailoring the content strategy to fit diverse user groups.

2. **Mapping the User Journey**: Constructing detailed maps of the user journey from the first contact to long-term engagement highlights essential content interaction points. These maps are crucial for placing strategic content that meets expectations at each phase of the user journey.

3. **Personalizing Content**: Tailoring content based on individual user actions significantly enhances user experience and satisfaction. Simple personalization can be as effective as advanced techniques, depending on the context and user data available.

```
// Simple personalization script
if (user.hasVisited('introPage')) {
  displayContent('additionalResources');
}
```

This snippet demonstrates basic personalization by modifying content delivery based on the user's browsing history, enhancing relevance and user engagement.

4. **Feedback Integration**: Incorporating user feedback mechanisms directly into the content strategy allows for real-time user input, which can steer content adjustments and enhancements.

5. **SEO Optimization**: Properly optimizing content for search engines ensures that it meets users' search intents and improves content discoverability. Thorough keyword research linked to user intent and incorporating those keywords naturally into content are fundamental SEO tactics.

6. **Focusing on Accessibility and Diversity**: Content should be designed to be accessible by all user segments, including those with disabilities. Adhering to standards like the Web Content Accessibility Guidelines (WCAG) and ensuring content reflects cultural and language diversity are critical for broad inclusivity.

```
<!-- Example of inclusive and accessible HTML content -->
<img src="community.jpg" alt="Photo of our community engagement">
<p lang="en-us">Our community engagement initiatives span the globe.</p>
```

This example uses an alt tag for visual content and specifies a language attribute to enhance accessibility and relevance for a global audience.

Evaluating Alignment Success

Continuously measuring the success of content alignment with user expectations is essential. Key performance indicators such as engagement rates, conversion rates, and user feedback should be regularly analyzed. Methods like A/B testing can provide empirical data to guide further content refinement.

Conclusion

Effective alignment of content strategy with user expectations is not merely about delivering content; it's about creating resonant user experiences that lead to sustained engagement and loyalty. By understanding user needs, implementing personalization, and ensuring inclusivity and accessibility, digital products can achieve greater relevance and success. Regular adjustments based on user feedback and analytics are crucial for maintaining this alignment and optimizing the overall user experience.

Chapter Twelve

Ethical Design and User Privacy

Principles of Ethical Design in UI/UX

Ethical design in UI/UX prioritizes creating interfaces that respect and enhance users' welfare, aligning with values that foster transparency, fairness, and integrity. This approach doesn't just make digital products functional—it makes them fair and respectful to users. This article outlines the core principles of ethical design in UI/UX and suggests methods for integrating these ideals into design practices effectively.

Overview of Ethical Design

Ethical design involves thoughtful decision-making in the digital product development process to positively affect users and society. It centers on benefiting users, safeguarding their rights, and enhancing their overall digital experience.

Key Principles of Ethical Design

1. **Prioritizing Privacy** Privacy protection is essential in ethical UI/UX design. It is imperative for designers to be transparent about how they collect and use data and to provide users with clear options for managing their personal information.

```
<!-- Example of a user-friendly privacy control interface -->
<label for="user-privacy">Select your privacy preferences:</label>
<select id="user-privacy" name="privacy">
   <option value="allow">Allow Data Sharing</option>
   <option value="deny" selected>Deny Data Sharing</option>
</select>
```

This example demonstrates how users can be given straightforward tools to manage their data privacy effectively, emphasizing respect for their preferences.

2. **Inclusivity** Ethical design ensures that digital products are accessible to all users, including those with disabilities. Compliance with accessibility standards such as the Web Content Accessibility Guidelines (WCAG) is critical for creating barrier-free designs.

```
<!-- Example of accessible button design -->
<button aria-label="Shut window" onclick="closeWindow()">X</button>
```

This design incorporates aria-label attributes to ensure that all users, especially those using assistive technologies, can navigate and utilize UI elements.

3. **Transparency and Honesty** Design transparency and honesty ensure that users are not misled by the interface. Ethical UI/UX design shuns deceptive practices, providing clear and straightforward information to help users make informed decisions.

4. **Sustainability** Considering the environmental impacts of digital product design, ethical designers aim to minimize negative effects and promote sustainability.

5. **Accountability** Designers must accept accountability for the social impacts of their designs. Implementing user feedback mechanisms is vital for this process.

```javascript
// Example of user feedback implementation
document.querySelector('#feedback-trigger').addEventListener('click', function() {
    activateFeedbackForm();
});
function activateFeedbackForm() {
    // Logic to display the feedback form
}
```

This JavaScript snippet shows how designers can provide users with an easy way to offer feedback, an important aspect of ethical accountability.

Implementing Ethical Principles

Effectively embedding ethical principles into UI/UX design involves several practical steps:

- **Ongoing Training**: Design teams should regularly receive training on ethical design principles to ensure these ideas are integrated into all facets of design.

- **Diverse User Testing**: Testing designs with a wide range of users helps ensure that products are inclusive and meet various user needs without being biased or exclusionary.

- **Formulate Ethical Guidelines**: Setting up clear ethical guidelines and review mechanisms helps maintain high ethical standards across all design projects.

Conclusion

Ethical design in UI/UX is crucial for developing digital products that are not just technically sound but also morally aligned with user welfare and societal good. By committing to principles such as privacy, inclusivity, transparency, sustainability, and accountability, designers can create products that truly respect and uplift users. Regular application of these principles is essential for cultivating trust and ensuring the enduring success of digital interfaces.

Incorporating Privacy by Design

Privacy by Design (PbD) is a critical methodology in today's technological landscape, designed to ensure that privacy is an integral part of the design process from the very beginning. Originally developed by Ann Cavoukian in the 1990s, PbD advocates for the inclusion of privacy features as foundational elements in technology systems, not as optional add-ons. For UI/UX designers, implementing PbD principles is vital to create products that genuinely protect user privacy, establish trust, and comply with legal standards.

Principles of Privacy by Design

PbD is governed by seven fundamental principles aimed at proactively embedding privacy into product design. These principles promote privacy assurance, user-centric practices, transparency, and comprehensive security measures throughout the entire lifecycle of the product.

Applying Privacy by Design in UI/UX

1. **Proactive Privacy Protections** Initiating privacy protections at the design stage means anticipating potential privacy risks and mitigating them before they become issues. This proactive approach is fundamental to PbD and involves integrating privacy-preserving measures early in the design process.

```
// Example: Proactive data encryption at the point of entry
function encryptDataImmediately(data) {
    const encrypted = CryptoJS.AES.encrypt(data, 'secure-key').toString();
    return encrypted;
}

document.getElementById('sensitive-input').addEventListener('input', function(event) {
    const encryptedData = encryptDataImmediately(event.target.value);
    // Use or store the encrypted data securely
});
```

This code snippet demonstrates encrypting data as it is entered, ensuring that user information is secured from the moment it is provided.

2. **Default Privacy Settings** Ensuring that privacy settings are configured to the most secure option by default is a core principle of PbD. This means users are automatically protected without needing to adjust their settings.

```
<!-- Example: Privacy-first approach in user settings -->
<label>
    <input type="checkbox" name="privacy_default" checked="false">
    Opt into data sharing.
</label>
```

140

In this example, data sharing is not enabled by default, requiring users to make an active choice to opt-in, which reinforces privacy by design.

3. **Robust Security from Start to Finish** Implementing comprehensive security measures from data collection through to its final disposition ensures that user information remains protected across all phases of its lifecycle.

4. **Transparent User Control** Providing clear, accessible information about how user data is used and offering straightforward mechanisms for users to control their personal information underscore transparency and user empowerment.

```html
<!-- Example: Transparent privacy controls interface -->
<button onclick="openPrivacyControls()">Configure Your Privacy Settings</button>

<script>
function openPrivacyControls() {
    // Display the user interface for privacy settings modification
}
</script>
```

This setup offers users easy access to adjust their privacy settings, enhancing their ability to manage their personal data effectively.

5. **Data Minimization** Limiting data collection to what is absolutely necessary for achieving the desired functionality of the application minimizes the risk of privacy breaches and reduces the scope of data management requirements.

Addressing Challenges

While the benefits of integrating PbD are significant, the approach can introduce challenges such as balancing user experience with stringent privacy controls. Addressing these challenges requires careful design consideration and ongoing engagement with privacy as a dynamic component of user interaction.

Conclusion

Incorporating Privacy by Design in UI/UX not only ensures compliance with privacy regulations but also builds a strong foundation of trust with users by demonstrating a commitment to safeguarding their personal information. By adopting PbD principles, designers and developers can create more secure, user-friendly, and privacy-conscious products that stand the test of time and user scrutiny.

Legal Considerations in Interface Design

Ensuring legal compliance in interface design is crucial not only for adhering to regulatory demands but also for building credibility with users and securing a product's market position. This discussion outlines essential legal considerations that UI/UX designers must account for when developing interfaces, providing strategies for effective integration of these elements.

Critical Legal Domains Affecting Interface Design

Several key legal areas impact interface design significantly, encompassing intellectual property, privacy regulations, accessibility mandates, and consumer protection laws. Mastery of these domains is crucial for creating compliant and user-friendly interfaces.

1. **Intellectual Property (IP)** IP laws protect original artistic and intellectual creations, which in UI/UX design, include elements like icons, custom graphics, and unique interface layouts. Designers are responsible for ensuring that their creations do not infringe on existing intellectual property and that any third-party content is used under proper licensing agreements.

```
<!-- Example of incorporating a licensed graphic with attribution -->
<img src="copyrighted-artwork.jpg" alt="Licensed graphic">
<p>Credit: [Artist's Name]</p>
```

This example demonstrates how to legally include copyrighted graphics in a design, ensuring proper attribution as required by IP laws.

2. **Privacy and Data Protection** With stringent privacy laws like the GDPR in Europe and the CCPA in California, it is essential for designers to integrate privacy safeguards directly into the interface. This includes clear mechanisms for user consent prior to data collection and transparent access to modify privacy preferences.

```
// Example of a compliant interface for user consent under GDPR
document.getElementById('privacy-policy-form').addEventListener('submit',
    function(event) {
    if (!document.getElementById('privacy-agreement-checkbox').checked) {
        event.preventDefault();
        alert('You must agree to the privacy policy to continue.');
    }
});
```

This JavaScript ensures compliance by verifying that users have actively consented to the privacy policy before proceeding, aligning with legal requirements for user data protection.

3. **Accessibility** Accessibility is mandated by laws like the ADA, which require that digital services be accessible to all users, including those with disabilities. This involves designing interfaces that are navigable and interpretable by technologies like screen readers.

```html
<!-- Example of an ADA-compliant form element -->
<label for="name-input">Name:</label>
<input type="text" id="name-input" aria-label="Enter your name" required>
```

By correctly labeling and incorporating ARIA attributes, this form element is made accessible, ensuring compliance with ADA guidelines.

4. **Consumer Protection** Laws in this category ensure that interfaces are designed to be fair and transparent, especially regarding pricing and service terms. Designers must ensure that all information is presented clearly to avoid misleading users.

```html
<!-- Example of clearly stating service terms -->
<div class="service-terms">
    Subscription Fee: $20/month <small>(Billed annually)</small>
</div>
```

This snippet clearly informs users of the billing terms associated with a subscription, fulfilling consumer protection requirements by avoiding potential confusion.

Strategies for Legal Compliance

To effectively integrate these legal considerations into UI/UX design, designers should:

- **Maintain Current Knowledge**: Regular updates on legal standards are essential for staying compliant.

- **Consult with Legal Experts**: Collaborative reviews with legal professionals can help preemptively identify and mitigate potential legal issues.

- **Perform Accessibility Evaluations**: Regular testing with users of varying abilities ensures the interface remains accessible.

- **Enhance Transparency**: Interfaces should be designed to make all necessary legal information easily accessible to users.

Conclusion

Integrating legal considerations into UI/UX design is vital for creating digital products that not only meet regulatory standards but also earn user trust and market acceptance. By addressing intellectual property, privacy, accessibility, and consumer protection comprehensively, designers can craft interfaces that are both innovative and compliant, ensuring their products stand up to legal scrutiny and user expectations.

Chapter Thirteen

Managing UX Projects

Advanced Project Management Tools and Techniques

Modern project landscapes demand the utilization of sophisticated project management tools and techniques to handle the complexities of contemporary projects efficiently. These advanced solutions improve project planning, enhance team collaboration, and streamline execution across diverse industries. Here we explore essential project management tools and methodologies that empower teams and managers to achieve exemplary project outcomes.

1. Agile Project Management

Agile project management is celebrated for its flexibility and emphasis on rapid, iterative cycles of development, known as sprints. It is particularly suited to projects where continuous adaptation to user feedback is vital. Notable Agile methodologies include:

- **Scrum**: Organizes work in short cycles or sprints, focusing on delivering incremental updates to products.

- **Kanban**: Employs visual boards to control the flow of work, aiming to optimize the process and reduce bottlenecks.

- **Lean**: Concentrates on delivering maximum value by identifying and eliminating all forms of process waste.

Platforms like Jira and Trello are designed to facilitate these Agile approaches, providing tools for managing backlogs, tracking sprints, and fostering team collaboration.

2. Hybrid Project Management

Hybrid project management blends traditional planning techniques such as the Waterfall method with the flexible, adaptive nature of Agile. This approach is beneficial for projects that require a mix of rigorous phase-based planning and dynamic adaptability.

- **Tools**: Tools like Microsoft Project and Smartsheet support hybrid methodologies by integrating detailed Gantt charts for structured planning alongside features that accommodate Agile practices.

3. Digital Collaboration Platforms

With remote work becoming more prevalent, powerful digital collaboration platforms have become indispensable. Tools like Slack, Microsoft Teams, and Asana merge communication with project management capabilities, ensuring that remote teams can work effectively regardless of geographical boundaries.

- **Features**: These tools offer functionalities such as task delegation, progress monitoring, and file sharing to enhance operational coordination.

4. Advanced Resource Management

Optimal resource management is critical to avoid resource over-allocation and maximize resource utilization. Advanced tools such as LiquidPlanner and Resource Guru provide robust features for tracking resource availability, scheduling, and budget management.

- **Technique**: Leveraging advanced analytics to project future resource requirements based on historical data can significantly improve resource allocation accuracy.

```python
# Python script for efficient resource allocation
def optimize_resource_allocation(tasks, resources):
    allocation_plan = {}
    for task in tasks:
        for resource in resources:
            if resource.remaining_hours >= task.needed_hours:
                allocation_plan[task.name] = resource.name
                resource.remaining_hours -= task.needed_hours
                break
    return allocation_plan

# Example implementation
project_tasks = [Task('Requirement Analysis', 80), Task('Implementation', 160)]
resources = [Resource('Alice Johnson', 240)]
print(optimize_resource_allocation(project_tasks, resources))
```

This Python script provides a straightforward approach to assigning resources to tasks based on availability, a key component in effective project management.

5. Risk Management Tools

Proactive risk management is essential for minimizing potential setbacks in project execution. Tools such as RiskyProject and nTask facilitate risk identification, impact analysis, and the development of mitigation strategies.

- **Technique**: Using Monte Carlo simulations within these tools helps predict a range of possible outcomes, aiding in the formulation of robust risk mitigation plans.

6. Real-Time Data and Reporting

The ability to monitor project status in real-time is crucial for modern project management. Integration with data visualization tools like Tableau and Power BI enables project managers to access live data streams and interactive reports.

- **Benefit**: Real-time reporting allows for quick decision-making and immediate response to project developments and challenges.

Conclusion

Advanced project management tools and techniques provide a range of functionalities that cater to the demands of modern, complex projects. Whether through employing Agile practices, utilizing hybrid approaches, or leveraging digital collaboration platforms, these tools help project managers and teams navigate the intricacies of project management effectively. By adopting these advanced solutions, organizations can ensure the successful delivery of projects in today's competitive and fast-paced project environments.

Collaborating and Communicating in Teams

In contemporary corporate environments, where teams may operate remotely or span several continents, mastering robust collaboration and communication is critical. Effective management of these distributed teams demands strategic communication approaches and meticulous coordination. This article explores essential techniques, digital tools, and best practices necessary for optimizing team interactions and ensuring effective communication within various organizational frameworks.

Foundations of Effective Team Collaboration

Optimal team collaboration extends beyond frequent interactions; it involves the orchestrated management of team dynamics, alignment towards common objectives, and the efficient harnessing of diverse skills within the team. Key elements crucial for successful collaboration include:

- **Team Diversity**: The variety in team composition can offer a rich pool of ideas and abilities, although it may also bring challenges such as differing communication styles and cultural variances.

- **Leadership Influence**: Leadership that emphasizes transparency, inclusiveness, and adaptability greatly improves collaborative efforts within a team.

- **Appropriate Communication Tools**: Effective team collaboration depends significantly on the selection of communication tools that adequately meet the project and team dynamics.

Strategies to Foster Team Collaboration

Enhancing team collaboration can be facilitated through several strategic initiatives:

1. **Clear Objectives and Defined Roles** Communicating clear objectives and defining distinct roles within the team help diminish confusion and align team members with the project's goals.

2. **Cultivation of Open Communication** Encouraging a culture that prizes open communication and consistent feedback can swiftly pinpoint and resolve issues, nurturing trust and open dialogue across the team.

3. **Adoption of Collaboration Technologies** Tools such as Slack, Microsoft Teams, and Zoom are essential for fostering effective communication, especially important in teams that are remote or geographically dispersed. These tools enable features like instant messaging, video conferencing, and simultaneous document editing.

```python
# Python code for automating reminder notifications via Slack
from slack_sdk import WebClient

slack_token = 'your-slack-api-token'
client = WebClient(token=slack_token)

def initiate_reminder(channel_id, message):
    client.chat_postMessage(channel=channel_id, text=message)

initiate_reminder('channel-id', "Reminder: Please prepare for the monthly
    strategy session at 2 PM.")
```

This script exemplifies how automating communication through a Slack bot can ensure that all team members receive timely reminders for critical meetings or events.

4. **Integration of Project Management Software** Utilizing software like Asana, Trello, and Monday.com

aids in task management, deadline monitoring, and keeping transparent communication regarding project milestones, ensuring that all members are consistently informed and engaged.

5. **Ongoing Refinement of Communication Practices** Continually evaluating and adjusting communication practices based on team feedback is essential for developing strategies that effectively address the unique needs of the team.

Communication Best Practices

Effective communication within teams is crucial and involves more than just the frequency of messages. Some best practices include:

- **Precision and Brevity**: Ensuring communications are both precise and brief can prevent miscommunications and ensure information is easily digestible.

- **Accommodation of Time Zones**: Scheduling communications to accommodate various time zones is crucial for global teams, ensuring all members can participate fully.

- **Consistent Updates and Meetings**: Regular updates and scheduled meetings help keep the team aligned on the project's progress and swiftly address any emerging challenges.

- **Efficient Feedback Mechanisms**: Implementing efficient mechanisms for both giving and receiving feedback is vital for maintaining team coherence and encouraging ongoing development.

Conclusion

Effectively navigating collaboration and communication is indispensable in modern workplaces, especially as teams become more diverse and projects increase in complexity. By employing strategic communication practices, leveraging sophisticated tools, and adhering to established best practices, teams can significantly enhance their productivity and successfully meet project objectives. Effective collaboration and communication are not only beneficial but necessary for thriving in today's dynamic and interconnected business environments.

Documenting UX Processes

In User Experience (UX) design, comprehensive documentation is a cornerstone that ensures clarity, accountability, and consistency across projects. Effective documentation not only aids in communicating the design process clearly but also helps in maintaining design fidelity, managing stakeholder expectations, and providing a reliable blueprint for future iterations. This article delves into the significance, techniques, and best practices in documenting UX processes effectively throughout the lifecycle of a project.

Importance of UX Documentation

Effective documentation in UX serves multiple essential purposes:

1. **Knowledge Distribution**: Proper documentation ensures that essential information is shared uniformly among current team members and future stakeholders.

2. **Collaboration Enhancement**: It serves as a crucial reference that can enhance understanding and cooperation among different project teams and disciplines.

3. **Consistency Preservation**: Documentation helps maintain design and user experience consistency across various project stages and team changes.

4. **Efficient Transitions**: Well-documented processes facilitate smoother transitions between different project phases or when shifting tasks between teams.

5. **Regulatory and Legal Compliance**: In some sectors, maintaining a detailed record of the UX process is necessary to comply with regulatory and legal standards.

Documentation Techniques in UX Processes

Documenting UX processes thoroughly involves capturing each phase of the design journey, from initial research to the final outputs. Key documentation components include:

1. **Project Outlines and Goals**: Documents that define the scope, objectives, and expected results of the project, accessible and regularly updated for all stakeholders.

2. **User Research Records**: All findings from user research activities like interviews, persona creation, and

usability tests should be meticulously documented. Tools such as Dovetail can be employed to organize and analyze this qualitative data effectively.

```python
# Example: Structuring user interview data for easy access and analysis
import json

feedback_records = [
    {"user_id": 101, "age": 30, "feedback": "The interface should be more user
        -friendly."},
    {"user_id": 102, "age": 42, "feedback": "The text needs to be larger for
        better readability."}
]

# Storing feedback in a JSON file for systematic analysis
with open('feedback_data.json', 'w') as file:
    json.dump(feedback_records, file, indent=4)
```

This snippet demonstrates organizing user feedback in a structured digital format, facilitating future analysis and reference.

3. **Design Annotations and Wireframes**: Comprehensive records of design specifications and annotated wireframes guide developers and new designers alike. Tools such as Sketch and Figma enable annotations and version control directly within design files.

4. **Test Results Documentation**: Documenting the outcomes and insights from usability testing sessions is crucial for backing design decisions and guiding subsequent iterations.

5. **Final Deliverables Documentation**: The final design documentation should include detailed mockups, interaction guidelines, and asset

specifications, often managed within design systems like Adobe XD or InVision, which integrate seamlessly with development tools.

Best Practices for Documenting UX Processes

To optimize the impact of UX documentation, adhere to these best practices:

- **Maintain Accessibility and Order**: Ensure that documents are easily accessible to all relevant parties and are organized logically.

- **Implement Version Control**: Accurate version control is crucial in environments where changes are frequent and multiple stakeholders are involved.

- **Prioritize Clarity**: Write documentation in clear, concise language to ensure it is understandable by stakeholders of various backgrounds.

- **Regularly Update Documents**: Documentation should evolve alongside the project to reflect new insights, decisions, and changes accurately.

Conclusion

Documenting UX processes is integral to the discipline of UX design, facilitating clearer communication, ensuring consistency, and simplifying project management. By implementing rigorous documentation practices and continuously updating these documents, UX teams can create a valuable resource that benefits the project's current scope and informs future developments. Effective documentation sets a solid foundation for success in both current projects and subsequent endeavors.

Chapter Fourteen

Preparing for the Future of UI/UX

Emerging Trends and Technologie

The rapid advancement of technology mandates that organizations keep abreast of the latest developments to maintain a competitive edge and adapt to the changing demands of consumers. This article discusses the major technological shifts and innovations currently transforming industries, including artificial intelligence (AI), quantum computing, and outlines their potential impacts on future business operations and societal evolution.

Artificial Intelligence and Machine Learning

Artificial Intelligence (AI) and Machine Learning (ML) continue to drive significant transformations across various sectors by automating operations, enhancing decision-making processes, and refining customer engagements. Prominent implementations include:

- **Automated Decision Processes**: AI is extensively used in financial sectors for streamlining credit scoring and in retail for optimizing inventory management.

- **Advancements in Natural Language Processing (NLP)**: Progress in NLP is equipping chatbots and digital assistants to manage more complex interactions, improving user experiences significantly.

- **Industrial Predictive Maintenance**: ML techniques are revolutionizing predictive maintenance by forecasting equipment failures in advance, thus minimizing downtime and enhancing operational efficiency.

Below is an example of implementing an ML model for predictive maintenance:

```python
from sklearn.ensemble import RandomForestClassifier
from sklearn.datasets import make_classification
from sklearn.model_selection import train_test_split

# Creating synthetic data for demonstration
X, y = make_classification(n_samples=1000, n_features=20, n_informative=2,
    n_redundant=10, random_state=42)
X_train, X_test, y_train, y_test = train_test_split(X, y, test_size=0.25,
    random_state=42)

# Setting up and training the random forest classifier
model = RandomForestClassifier(n_estimators=100, random_state=42)
model.fit(X_train, y_train)

# Testing the model's performance
accuracy = model.score(X_test, y_test)
print("Accuracy of the model:", accuracy)
```

This Python code snippet demonstrates how a RandomForest classifier is utilized to classify data, a method applicable to predictive maintenance by training on relevant operational data.

Internet of Things (IoT)

The Internet of Things (IoT) is drastically expanding its influence, enhancing device connectivity and intelligence across consumer and industrial sectors:

- **Enhancements in Smart Home Technology**: IoT is transforming home management by enabling automated control over appliances, thus improving energy efficiency and security.

- **Industrial Internet of Things (IIoT)**: IoT technologies in industrial contexts are improving data collection and analysis, leading to optimized operations and better decision-making.

Blockchain Technology

Blockchain is finding applications far beyond its initial use in cryptocurrencies, offering robust, transparent transaction capabilities across various fields:

- **Enhancing Supply Chain Management**: With blockchain, every step of the supply chain is recorded in a tamper-proof ledger, improving transparency and efficiency.

- **Smart Contracts**: Blockchain supports smart contracts that execute automatically when predetermined conditions are met, thereby enhancing efficiency in sectors such as real estate and contractual agreements.

Quantum Computing

Quantum computing is emerging as a revolutionary technology capable of solving complex problems that are currently beyond the reach of classical computers:

- **Pharmaceutical Development**: Quantum computing could vastly accelerate the drug development process by enabling the precise simulation of molecular interactions.

- **Next-Generation Cryptography**: It is set to develop advanced cryptographic techniques that provide security measures robust enough to counter quantum computing threats.

5G Technology

The deployment of 5G technology is set to revolutionize telecommunications, offering unprecedented data speeds and network reliability, supporting advanced mobile broadband and IoT applications:

- **Superior Mobile Broadband (eMBB)**: 5G will facilitate extremely rapid data transmission, enhancing experiences with high-resolution streaming and downloads.

- **Critical Real-Time Communications (URLLC)**: 5G is crucial for applications that require instantaneous data exchange, such as in automated driving and remote healthcare.

Implications for the Future

The continuous evolution of these technologies brings both vast opportunities and significant challenges. Companies must consider effective integration strategies, address potential skill shortages, and manage the socio-economic impacts of automation and digital security concerns.

Engaging with these technological trends is essential for any organization striving for innovation and market leadership. By adopting and integrating these emerging trends, businesses can effectively manage digital transformation complexities and position themselves for enduring success in an ever-evolving market landscape.

Preparing for Advanced Topics in UI/UX

As the fields of User Interface (UI) and User Experience (UX) design continually progress, staying ahead requires designers to deepen their knowledge and skills in complex areas. This guide discusses the necessary steps for UI/UX designers to enhance their expertise and readiness for high-level projects, emphasizing the integration of the latest design practices and technologies.

Enhancing Core Design Skills

It's essential for designers to first solidify their understanding of fundamental UI/UX principles. Proficiency in areas such as visual design, user-centered design, interaction design, and information architecture is indispensable. These skills provide the groundwork for tackling more intricate design challenges.

Keeping Pace with Industry Evolution

The UI/UX landscape is ever-changing, making it vital to stay informed and connected:

- **Ongoing Education**: Advanced training through specialized courses and workshops is crucial. Platforms like Coursera, Udemy, and LinkedIn Learning offer resources tailored to complex UX research techniques and innovative design processes.

- **Community Engagement**: Active participation in UI/UX forums, attending industry conferences, and engaging in seminars are excellent ways to stay updated on new trends and network with other professionals.

- **Regular Reading**: Keeping up with publications such as "Smashing Magazine," "UX Magazine," and reports from the Nielsen Norman Group ensures that designers are aware of the latest research and best practices.

Advanced Research and Testing Techniques

Complex UI/UX projects require sophisticated approaches to research and testing:

- **Eye Tracking Analysis**: Using eye tracking technology helps quantify user interaction with interfaces, identifying where users focus their attention.

- **Detailed A/B Testing**: Implement detailed A/B testing to scientifically determine the best design elements that resonate with users.

- **Predictive Analytics Implementation**: Harnessing predictive analytics can help foresee user actions, enhancing the ability to tailor personalized experiences.

Example configuration for A/B testing with Google Analytics:

```python
# Python example for setting up an A/B test using Google Analytics
from google.analytics.data_v1beta import BetaAnalyticsDataClient
from google.analytics.data_v1beta.types import DateRange, Entity, Metric,
    Dimension, RunReportRequest

client = BetaAnalyticsDataClient()

# Define A/B test details
request = RunReportRequest(
    entity=Entity(property_id='YOUR_PROPERTY_ID'),
    dimensions=[Dimension(name='eventName')],
    metrics=[Metric(name='activeUsers')],
    date_ranges=[DateRange(start_date='2022-01-01', end_date='2022-01-31')]
)

# Execute A/B test to compare user engagement with different UI designs
response = client.run_report(request)
print(response)
```

This Python code example demonstrates setting up an A/B test using the Google Analytics API, useful for assessing user engagement across different UI variations.

Integrating Emerging Technologies

To stay competitive, embracing new technologies like augmented reality (AR), virtual reality (VR), artificial intelligence (AI), and voice user interfaces (VUIs) is essential:

- **AR and VR Development**: Designers should explore the unique challenges of creating interfaces in immersive AR and VR environments.

- **AI-Enhanced Designs**: Using AI to automate and personalize user experiences offers a significant advantage in creating responsive designs.

- **Voice-Driven Interfaces**: As voice interaction becomes more prevalent, learning to design effective voice commands and feedback is crucial.

Promoting a Culture of Innovation

Innovative design solutions arise from a culture that values creativity and problem-solving. Design thinking is key, emphasizing brainstorming, prototyping, and iterative development, which encourage out-of-the-box thinking and solution-oriented designs.

Conclusion

Advanced UI/UX design demands more than just technical skills; it requires a commitment to lifelong learning and an openness to innovation. By reinforcing foundational knowledge, staying updated with the latest industry trends, employing advanced research methods, embracing cutting-edge technologies, and fostering a culture of creativity, UI/UX designers can effectively navigate complex challenges and lead in the creation of compelling, user-centered designs.

Continuous Learning and Adaptation

In the swiftly evolving landscape of UI/UX design, staying committed to ongoing learning and being adaptable is essential. As technology progresses and the expectations of users advance, UI/UX practitioners must keep sharpening their abilities and modifying their approaches.

The Critical Importance of Continuous Learning

For UI/UX professionals, continuous learning entails a combination of organized educational programs and individual exploration. With the rapid pace of technological change, it's crucial for designers to continually enhance their capabilities and update their knowledge.

Formal Education and Training: Lifelong learning through updated courses and certifications is critical. Learning platforms like Coursera and Udemy provide cutting-edge courses on topics like the integration of artificial intelligence in UX and sophisticated data analysis. For instance, a course like "Machine Learning for Designers" could involve practical application exercises using Python to delve into user behavior data, aiding in more informed design decisions.

```python
# Python example for processing user behavior data
import pandas as pd
import numpy as np
from sklearn.cluster import KMeans

# Reading user interaction data
data = pd.read_csv('user_interactions.csv')

# Normalizing the data
normalized_data = (data - data.mean()) / data.std()

# Applying K-means clustering to discern patterns
kmeans = KMeans(n_clusters=4)
clusters = kmeans.fit_predict(normalized_data)

# Assigning cluster labels to the data for further analysis
data['Cluster'] = clusters
print(data.groupby('Cluster').mean())
```

Conferences and Workshops: Engaging in industry-specific events like the UX Design Conference or Adobe MAX provides invaluable exposure to novel ideas and technologies, supplemented with practical workshop experience.

Peer Collaboration and Networking: Regular interactions with fellow professionals through platforms and forums are crucial for staying current with rapid industry changes and adopting new best practices.

The Necessity of Adaptation in UI/UX Design

Staying adaptable is vital for UI/UX professionals, requiring them to keep pace with new technologies and adjust to evolving user demands. This adaptability is evident across various dimensions:

Technology Adaptation: Designers need to assimilate new tools into their workflow seamlessly. For example, the emergence of no-code platforms like Webflow has transformed the ways in which prototypes are developed, facilitating quicker iterations and better collaboration.

Methodological Adaptation: With the continual evolution of design methodologies, designers must remain agile, incorporating swift prototyping and feedback loops into their practices.

Cognitive Adaptation: Designers are tasked with foreseeing and catering to user needs, often before they become explicit, applying their deep understanding of behavioral psychology.

Strategies for Successful Adaptation

UI/UX designers can enhance their adaptability by employing several effective strategies:

1. **Setting Learning Goals**: Identifying specific development areas and establishing measurable goals can help direct learning efforts.

2. **Creating a Learning Schedule**: Allocating regular time for educational activities ensures steady personal and professional growth.

3. **Feedback Mechanisms**: Actively seeking and applying feedback from peers, mentors, and users is critical for identifying areas for enhancement and promoting a culture of ongoing learning.

To sum up, for UI/UX designers, embracing continuous learning and adaptation is not just beneficial—it's essential. Keeping up with technological advancements, adapting to new methodologies, and preempting user needs not only bolsters a designer's capabilities but also propels the entire UI/UX field forward. This perpetual cycle of learning and adapting is what keeps the discipline exciting and vital to the success of digital initiatives.

Conclusion

Summarizing Key Insights and Skills Gained

In the field of UI/UX design, summarizing key insights and skills is a pivotal exercise that reflects a designer's professional growth and preparedness for tackling increasingly complex challenges. This reflective summary serves as a comprehensive review, documenting the transition from foundational knowledge to specialized skills and highlighting the impact of these skills on future projects and innovations within the field.

Mastery of Foundational UI/UX Skills

The journey of a UI/UX designer typically begins with mastering fundamental skills such as understanding visual design principles, developing empathy for users, and grasping interface layout techniques. As a designer's career progresses, these basic skills are expanded upon through applied projects and continuous learning. For instance, initial skills in color theory and layout are essential, but with experience, integrating these with advanced user research and analytics becomes crucial.

Technical skills also evolve, starting from proficiency in basic design tools like Adobe XD or Sketch to more complex software and methodologies that involve integrating user data into the design process. A solid grasp of programming, particularly in languages like JavaScript or Python, enhances a designer's ability to tailor user interfaces based on data-driven insights.

```
# Python script for basic text analysis of user feedback
import pandas as pd

# Loading user feedback
feedback_data = pd.read_csv('user_feedback.csv')

# Identifying frequent feedback themes
feedback_themes = feedback_data['comments'].value_counts().head(10)
print("Top feedback themes:", feedback_themes)

# Function to modify design elements based on user feedback
def modify_design(element, adjustment):
    print(f"Modifying {element} to {adjustment}")

# Applying modifications based on feedback
modify_design('button_color', 'increase_contrast')
```

Deepening User-Centered Design Practices

As they gain experience, UI/UX designers increasingly focus on integrating user-centered design principles more deeply within every phase of product development. This involves not only considering the user in design decisions but also engaging them directly through participatory design, iterative testing, and constant feedback. An important realization for advanced practitioners is viewing user feedback as an ongoing, dialogic process that is integral to refining design decisions.

This approach might include sophisticated user testing techniques like A/B testing, or employing machine learning algorithms to anticipate and respond to user behaviors, thus crafting more intuitive and adaptive user interfaces.

Leveraging Emerging Technologies

A significant aspect of a designer's skill progression is the ability to adopt and implement cutting-edge technologies. From augmented reality (AR) and virtual reality (VR) to advanced voice user interfaces, adept designers must not only keep abreast of these innovations but also harness them to enhance user experiences. This often requires learning new programming languages or engagement with platforms that are outside traditional UI/UX design paradigms, such as Unity for AR/VR interfaces.

The rapid assimilation and practical application of new technologies in projects highlight a designer's flexibility and innovative spirit. Such capabilities are often honed through dedicated training, participation in technology-focused hackathons, or through collaborative ventures that explore new frontiers in UI/UX design.

Conclusion: Envisioning a Future-Proof UI/UX Career

In conclusion, summarizing the key insights and skills gained in the journey of a UI/UX designer outlines a path of substantial professional development from basic design principles to advanced, strategic design thinking. The amalgamation of deep technical knowledge with core design skills enables designers to craft personalized, dynamic, and user-centric experiences. Moreover, the proactive adoption of new technologies prepares designers for future innovations in the field.

This reflective practice not only highlights a designer's individual growth and adaptability but also contributes to the collective advancement of the UI/UX profession, fostering a culture of perpetual learning and continuous improvement.

The Continuous Path of UI/UX Mastery

The journey to mastering UI/UX design is a relentless pursuit that demands a deep and ongoing engagement with evolving technologies, user behaviors, and design innovations. It requires more than a foundational understanding of design principles; mastery is about creating experiences that resonate deeply with users, both functionally and emotionally.

Building Advanced Design Skills

At the foundation of UI/UX mastery are essential design skills such as effective layout creation, sophisticated use of color, and strategic typography application. These elements are critical for crafting interfaces that not only look good but also perform well. However, true mastery involves a deeper level of engagement—proactively understanding and predicting user needs through a blend of qualitative and quantitative research.

Experienced UI/UX designers often employ advanced data analysis techniques to extract meaningful insights from user data. This can include using machine learning tools to detect patterns and behaviors that inform targeted design improvements. For instance, employing Python to conduct data analyses can reveal user preferences and pain points, directly impacting design decisions.

```
# Python script for detailed user behavior analysis
import pandas as pd
from sklearn.preprocessing import StandardScaler
from sklearn.decomposition import PCA

# Importing and normalizing user interaction data
user_interaction_data = pd.read_csv('interaction_data.csv')
scaler = StandardScaler()
normalized_data = scaler.transform(user_interaction_data)

# Using PCA to extract principal behavioral factors
pca = PCA(n_components=2)
pca_results = pca.transform(normalized_data)
analysis_df = pd.DataFrame(pca_results, columns=['Behavioral Factor 1',
    'Behavioral Factor 2'])

print("Detailed Insights from User Behavior Analysis:", analysis_df.head())
```

Dedication to Lifelong Learning

The landscape of UI/UX design tools and methodologies is continuously changing. Masters of the craft must keep pace with these developments by embracing the latest design software that integrates AI functionalities and learning new programming languages to enhance interactive capabilities.

Additionally, a masterful UI/UX designer is committed to refining their designs through iterative processes, constantly incorporating user feedback to optimize the user experience. This requires routine user testing and updating designs based on the insights gathered.

Navigating Specialization and Broadening Expertise

As they progress, UI/UX designers may choose to specialize in specific design areas such as mobile UX, voice user interfaces, or immersive technologies like AR/VR. Specialization allows for deep diving into specific content areas, providing detailed expertise that enhances the quality of specialized projects.

Alternatively, broadening one's scope to encompass related fields such as front-end development, psychology, or strategic content planning can provide a comprehensive perspective on product development and user engagement, enriching a designer's ability to make strategic decisions.

Advancing into Leadership Roles

Achieving high levels of mastery often propels designers into leadership positions. In these roles, they not only apply their deep technical skills but also lead design teams and shape project strategies. Effective leadership in UI/UX design involves advocating for user-centric approaches and influencing organizational design thinking.

Masters of UI/UX also contribute significantly to the growth of the field through education, research, and public speaking. Sharing knowledge and insights not only establishes them as thought leaders but also drives the field forward by introducing new ideas and promoting innovation.

Conclusion

The path to UI/UX mastery is lifelong and characterized by constant learning, skill enhancement, and leadership. It compels designers to remain at the forefront of technological and design advancements, pushing the boundaries to anticipate and influence the future direction of user experiences. Through this relentless pursuit, seasoned UI/UX professionals not only advance their own careers but also drive substantial progress within the broader design community.

Encouragement to Experiment and Innovate

In the UI/UX design landscape, fostering a culture of experimentation and innovation is crucial for advancing the discipline and developing solutions that resonate deeply with users. This approach not only leads to the creation of trailblazing designs but also ensures these innovations effectively tackle user challenges.

The Critical Role of Experimentation in UI/UX Design

Experimentation is key in UI/UX design, serving as a vital testbed for validating new concepts and refining strategies based on direct feedback from real-world usage. This practice enables designers to test their theories, optimize interfaces, and improve user engagement through continual refinement. Experimentation goes beyond merely testing known variables; it's about discovering innovative methods that can significantly enhance user interactions.

For example, running A/B tests on different interface designs to determine which yields better user engagement or conversion rates is a common practice. Below is a basic Python script to help analyze data from such tests:

```
import pandas as pd
from scipy.stats import ttest_ind

# Loading data from an A/B testing campaign
ab_data = pd.read_csv('ab_test_data.csv')

# Splitting the data into groups according to the test variant
group_a = ab_data[ab_data['variant'] == 'A']['conversion']
group_b = ab_data[ab_data['variant'] == 'B']['conversion']

# Using a t-test to evaluate the effectiveness of the two variants
stat, p_value = ttest_ind(group_a, group_b)

print(f"Testing Results: Statistic: {stat}, P-value: {p_value}")
```

This snippet provides a way to use statistical analysis to guide decisions about which design elements are more effective based on actual user responses.

Building an Environment for Innovation

Creating a culture that actively supports innovation involves more than just encouragement. It necessitates practical steps such as setting aside times for brainstorming, allocating resources for experimental projects, and establishing innovation centers where creative ideas can be explored without immediate financial repercussions.

Utilizing frameworks like Design Thinking can greatly enhance this culture. This approach prioritizes understanding users through empathy, supports rapid prototyping, and stresses iterative feedback, aligning innovations closely with both user expectations and organizational objectives.

Harnessing Technology to Drive Innovation

New technological tools continuously redefine the potential for creativity in UI/UX design. Advanced software that integrates

AI and machine learning not only streamlines the design process but also opens up deeper insights into user behaviors. This enables the development of more personalized and adaptive user interfaces. Consider the following example where machine learning predicts user preferences to adjust the UI dynamically:

```python
from sklearn.ensemble import RandomForestClassifier
from sklearn.model_selection import train_test_split
import pandas as pd

# Loading data from user interactions
user_data = pd.read_csv('user_data.csv')

# Preparing the data for modeling
input_features = user_data.drop('user_preference', axis=1)
output_labels = user_data['user_preference']

# Dividing the data into training and testing sets
X_train, X_test, y_train, y_test = train_test_split(input_features, output_labels
    , test_size=0.2, random_state=50)

# Training a RandomForest classifier
forest_model = RandomForestClassifier(n_estimators=100)
forest_model.fit(X_train, y_train)

# Using the trained model to predict user preferences
predictions = forest_model.predict(X_test)

print(f"Predicted User Preferences: {predictions}")
```

Overcoming Obstacles to Innovation

Innovation can be stifled by various barriers, including budget constraints, strict project timelines, or a culture averse to risk. To overcome these challenges, it is important to cultivate an environment where experimentation is valued, innovative efforts are recognized, and there is a systematic approach for implementing creative ideas.

Conclusion

Promoting a spirit of experimentation and innovation in UI/UX design is essential for staying at the forefront of the industry and effectively meeting user needs. It requires creating a supportive organizational culture, leveraging cutting-edge technologies, and crafting strategies to overcome barriers to innovation. By adopting this proactive approach, organizations can continually evolve and deliver exceptional, innovative user experiences.